European Mythology

LIBRARY OF THE WORLD'S
MYTHS AND LEGENDS

European Mythology

Jacqueline Simpson

PETER BEDRICK BOOKS
NEW YORK

Half-title. A Breton wood-carving which captures the stereotyped image of a witch: old, ugly, accompanied by a cat, and busy grinding herbs for her potions. The Wellcome Historical Medical Museum, London.

Frontispiece. The Round Table in Castle Hall, Winchester. Radiocarbon analysis dates it to the fourteenth century; probably it was made on the orders of Edward III, who announced in 1344 that he would found an order of knights modelled on Arthur's Company of the Round Table. Its decoration is later; it displays a Tudor Rose, and the portrait of 'Arthur' seems to be a youthful Henry VIII.

First American edition published in 1987 by Peter Bedrick Books, New York.
European Mythology first published in 1987 by The Hamlyn Publishing Group Limited, London.
Published by agreement with The Hamlyn Publishing Group Limited

Library of Congress Cataloging-in-Publication Data
Simpson, Jacqueline.
  European mythology.
  Includes index.
  1. Folklore—Europe. I. Title.
GR135.S56   1987   398'.094   86-22266

ISBN 0-87226-044-5

Printed in Hong Kong

Contents

Folklore: A Window on the Past

Folk Beliefs: The Myths of a Sub-Culture

The title of this book needs some explanation. My predecessors in this series have dealt with Greek, Roman, Celtic and Scandinavian mythologies, so readers may well wonder what, when these major fields have been covered, can still remain to be called *European Mythology*? They may then be further puzzled to see that the topics I shall be discussing are drawn from folk beliefs, customs and folktales, since it is commonly assumed that 'mythology' and 'folklore' are mutually exclusive categories. Their differences can be viewed from many angles. Myths are, by definition, about gods and semi-divine heroes, whereas folktales are chiefly about humans, even if endowed with supernatural powers; myths usually are linked into a coherent system, whereas folklore is more fragmented; myths are sacred to their tellers, and sometimes linked to ritual, but folktales are secular; myths are endorsed by the dominant social groups (rulers and priests), but the term 'folklore' is generally applied to a sub-culture existing independently of, or even in opposition to, the culture of the élite. The distinction is even sharper when, as is often the case, myths are being compared not with folktales in general (many of which embody seriously held beliefs), but with one particular genre, the fairytale, which is almost always told simply for its entertainment value, and is nowadays frequently aimed only at an audience of children. Is it not therefore paradoxical to include a book on European folklore in a series on mythology?

The distinction, however, is less rigid than it first seems. For one thing, many story-patterns and their component elements ('motifs') are equally common in folktales and in myths – visits to the Otherworld, for instance, or magical transformations, or dragon-slaying. More importantly, many folk beliefs are just as seriously concerned as myths are with explaining the mysteries of life, death and the universe. Folklore, like mythology, describes supernatural beings affecting good and bad luck, bringing blessings, or causing disease and death; it deals with the Otherworld, and ghosts; with human beings who allegedly communicate with and control these supernatural beings; with the origins of the world and of individual creatures and objects in it. Folklore can sometimes be associated with rituals to procure supernatural results, just as some myths are; this is rare in present-day Europe, but one clear example is the dance of exorcism which Romanian *cǎlusari* perform to heal people afflicted by evil fairies (see pp. 121–6). Other customs, now vaguely said to 'bring luck', may once have had similarly explicit aims. Some types of folklore are even regarded as 'sacred' by their practitioners; thus, words and actions used in healing and exorcizing are often kept secret, and healers may observe various taboos and rituals to purify themselves before exercising their art. Perhaps only the sociological differentiation between myth and folklore is universally valid, since it is a convention built into the words themselves. When a

Opposite. A well at Youlgreave, Derbyshire, dressed with a design in flowers at Ascensiontide, 1982. The subjects chosen for the designs are always Christian, but it is possible (though unprovable) that the custom derives from pre-Christian reverence for water sources.

scholar observes a system of beliefs endorsed by a whole society, including its élite, he calls it a 'mythology' (or, if he respects it, a 'religion'); but if it belongs only to a sub-group, especially a less educated or less privileged group, he labels it 'folklore'.

The subject-matter of this book is indeed 'folklore' in this sense, as it came chiefly from low-status sub-groups (usually peasant communities), and frequently lacked approval from churches, intellectuals, and ruling classes. Yet it is a 'mythology' in that it is concerned with supernatural forces as real entities, to be reckoned with in the everyday world, and not just as material for entertaining or edifying fantasies (as in fairytales or fables). And it is 'European' because its main features are pretty consistent throughout Europe, despite political and linguistic barriers; the range of activities ascribed to fairies, for instance, remains much the same everywhere, whatever names they are known by. Admittedly, the whole corpus of folk-belief and folk-custom cannot be observed in its entirety at any one period and place; recording in earlier centuries was very haphazard, and the uneven pace of modernization in the nineteenth and twentieth centuries destroyed traditions in some regions while elsewhere they still flourished. Nevertheless, there are many

cases where a point can equally well be illustrated by examples from Norway or Switzerland, Russia or France, and readers should not assume that a country named here is the *only* one where a particular story or belief occurs; to produce a proper distribution analysis of European folklore would need a book many times larger than this. I have also often deliberately selected Continental examples rather than British or Irish ones, which are more easily accessible to anyone wanting to make comparisons.

But why did European peasants need folklore to formulate their concepts of the supernatural? Surely Christianity explained all problems from the origin of the world to the fate of the dead; surely God, Christ, Mary, saints, angels and devils could suffice to account for every blessing or misfortune in life? The two systems did not necessarily conflict at every point – indeed, there were many links between them, as later chapters will show – but the persistence of sub-Christian and non-Christian ideas must indicate that folklore satisfied some needs which Christianity failed to meet. Social historians such as Keith Thomas in England, Le Roy Ladurie in France and Ernesto de Martino in Italy have addressed this problem, producing rich results for places and times where adequate documentation exists. I would

tentatively hazard a few general considerations. First, Christianity sharply polarizes the supernatural into good and evil beings; folk beliefs add a range of ambiguous, capricious, 'neutral' beings, whose unpredictable activities correspond more closely to the arbitrary way good and bad luck actually occur. Secondly, Christianity often teaches a resigned acceptance of misfortunes; folklore offers magical ways of counteracting malevolent witches and fairies who are blamed for the misfortunes, and this self-help system may have been psychologically more encouraging than prayer. Thirdly, even Catholicism, with its plethora of local saints and shrines, could not confer importance upon every village and every stretch of countryside; local legends, however, which are a ubiquitous form of folktale, reflect the countryman's pride in the unique importance of his own neighbourhood.

The reactions of the élite to folk culture vary greatly at different periods, and also according to which aspect of it is under discussion. At some epochs, church authorities (whether Catholic or Protestant) denounce folk 'superstitions' and accuse folk festivals of encouraging drunkenness and sexuality; at others, piety and folklore blend harmoniously, creating a picturesque saint's cult – or a disastrous obsession

with witch-hunting. The relation of science to folklore fluctuates too; much that was acceptable at all levels of society in the seventeenth century was mocked as 'old wives' tales' in the nineteenth, while some traditional items of folk medicine are now once again thought worth investigating. At some periods, notably in the Middle Ages and the nineteenth century, poets, dramatists and novelists have seized upon themes from folklore and exploited their romantic, exotic, or horrific qualities, transmitting into the mainstream of European literature their versions of fairyland, ghosts, vampires, witchcraft, and the like, or of individual figures such as Arthur, Faust, or Gargantua. These literary borrowings are unfortunately often accompanied by distortion; sometimes this takes the form of nostalgia and prettification (as in much writing on the topic of fairies), and sometimes of commercial sensationalism of the macabre (as in many current novels and films).

Almost always, however, educated people who were aware of folk culture realized that it was old, and deep-rooted. Sometimes this increased their disapproval. Medieval Catholic writers condemned such customs as decorating trees and wells as relics of pagan idolatry, and insisted on identifying fairies with demons. Protestants later took the same line, and added a determination to root out all traces of Catholicism, which some considered practically the same as paganism. The Rev. Henry Bourne, discussing the decoration of wells in his *Antiquitates Vulgares* (1725), wrote:

There need be no Question, but as this Custom is practically Heathenish, so it is also originally: For the Heathens were wont to worship Streams and Fountains, and to suppose that the Nymphs, whom they imagined to be Goddesses of the Waters, presided over them. As the Papists have borrowed many of their silly and superstitious Ceremonies from the Religion of the Heathens, so in this particular, a sottish, stupid, and abominable Custom, they could borrow no where else. For we had no such Custom, neither at any Time the Churches of GOD.

Other antiquarians took a more sympathetic view of the old rural culture, though even John Aubrey (1626-97) comments with some embarassment upon his fondness for collecting information about customs and legends:

Old Customs and old wives' fables are grosse things, but yet ought not to be buried in Oblivion; there may be some truth and usefulnesse to be picked out of them, besides 'tis a pleasure to consider the Errours that enveloped former Ages: as also the present.

Both passages are cited in R. M. Dorson, *The British Folklorists: A History*, London, 1968, p. 12.

The Search for Origins

By the nineteenth century, scholars engaged in collecting and studying folklore were systematically seeking evidence to illuminate those periods of European history and prehistory for which little or no written records remained. By investigating peasant culture and tracing the origins of its most archaic traits, they hoped to rediscover the mental attitudes of long vanished epochs, thus opening a window on to the past. The contemporary countryman was not studied for his own sake; the focus of interest was on his ancestors.

Frequently, this endeavour was motivated by nationalist fervour. The influential eighteenth-century thinker Johann von Herder had argued that each nation had an identity, a 'soul', which found its purest expression in the 'natural' poetry of illiterate creators—the unknown composers and transmitters of epics, ballads, and folk songs. His teachings inspired several generations of researchers, especially in countries where a political struggle to achieve unity and/or independence from foreign domination reinforced the concept of a 'national soul'. The Greeks, for instance, had been angered by the allegations of some nineteenth-century German and Austrian writers that they were no true descendants of the Classical Greeks, but a mongrel blend of Slavs and Levantines; in reply, patriotic scholars led by Nicholas Polites (1852-1921) and Stilpon Kyriakides (1887-1964) turned to folklore for evidence of racial and cultural continuity. Using evidence from peasant tales and songs, they proved that the modern death demon, Charos, preserved the name and attributes of Charon; that female spirits of hills, streams and woods, now known collectively as *Neraides*, correspond to various categories of nymph in Classical mythology; that the modern mermaid resembles the Classical siren, even though she is confusingly called a *Gorgona*.

Jacob and Wilhelm Grimm also set out to recover cultural traits from distant times—in their case, from the pre-literate past common to all nations of Germanic stock. Just as Jacob Grimm, and others, had successfully reconstructed the extinct languages of Primitive Germanic and Indo-European by comparing the shared vocabulary of their descendants, so he and his brother aspired to reconstruct the beliefs and customs of the closely linked Germanic tribes at the start of the Dark Ages, and thus pinpoint their characteristic national ethos. One of Jacob Grimm's major scholarly achievements was his *Deutsche Mythologie* (1835), in which he assembled a mass of contemporary folklore data bearing traces of old cults, myths and rituals, and compared them to the explicit pre-Christian mythology

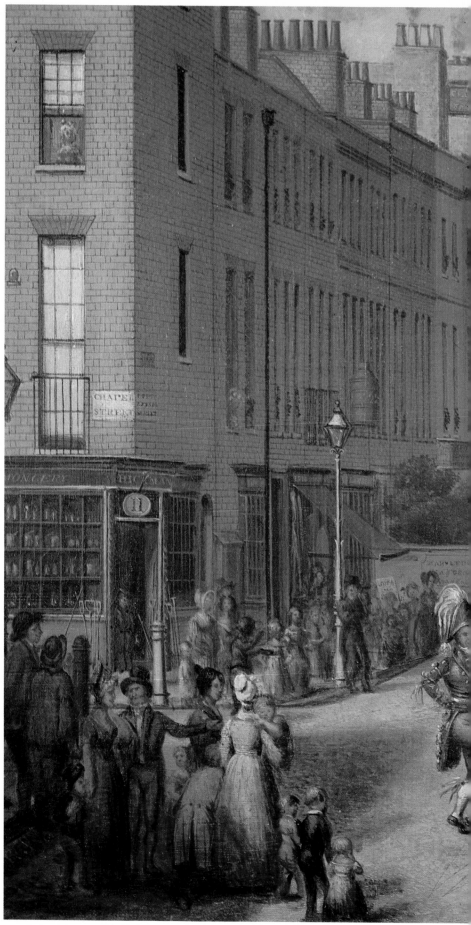

The Jack-in-the-Green, London c. 1837-47. A group of sweeps in fancy dress, including a 'lord', a 'lady', and a clown, dance round the Jack hidden in his leaf-covered frame. In the foreground, one 'climbing boy' collects money from onlookers, while another clatters his shovel and brush. Museum of London.

preserved in medieval writings such as the Icelandic Eddas. His work in this field has largely stood the test of time. There would be less agreement nowadays with the further claim, enthusiastically expressed by Wilhelm Grimm, that fairytales too are 'the remains of an ancient faith extending far back into the oldest times, in which spiritual things are expressed in a figurative manner'.

Meanwhile a group of British scholars (now known as the 'evolutionary' or 'anthropological' folklorists) argued that folklore was the key to a past far more remote than Germanic tribes or Classical Greece. Their method was to seek parallels between the isolated and apparently meaningless irrational beliefs and customs found in Europe and those of so-called 'savages'–the indigenous peoples of Africa, Australia, Polynesia and the Americas–in whose societies similar items formed part of an integrated thought-system. These parallels were held to prove that the European data were 'survivals' from some very remote period when Europeans were at the same cultural level as the 'savages'; by investigating survivals one could penetrate the earliest phase of our history. The goal, and the method, were formulated by Edward B. Tylor in his *Primitive Culture* (1871); they dominated the work of Andrew Lang, Edward Clodd, E. S. Hartland and many other late nineteenth-century English folklorists, and became universally known through Sir James Frazer's *The Golden Bough*. This famous book first appeared in 1890, and gradually expanded into twelve volumes; a single-volume abridgement came out in 1922. So great was its influence that Frazer's theories are still often regarded by the general public as proven facts, for instance the idea that harvest customs are relics of human sacrifices to ensure the success of the crops, or that it had once been normal procedure for aging kings to be killed off before their strength failed.

Underlying all the work of Tylor, Frazer and their associates is a fundamental assumption that all societies evolve through the same stages. Tylor stressed the sequence from savagery to barbarism to civilization, and Frazer that from magic to religion to science, but both thought it perfectly valid to use data from present-day 'savages' to explain the sources of European folklore. Their procedure, however, is now rejected by anthropologists as unsound, since it is realized that the development of societies is by no means uniform, that superficially similar items may have profoundly different significances in their respective social settings, and that even the most seemingly 'primitive' society is itself the result of centuries of evolution and cannot be taken as representing, unchanged, the way of life of much earlier epochs.

In their eagerness to uncover archaic

material, the evolutionary folklorists frequently deliberately ignored any element in a belief or custom which reflected medieval or post-medieval influences, seeing it as a corruption or irrelevancy not worth serious study. This could lead to serious distortion, since elements from diverse sources and periods are closely interwoven in folk culture, and the investigator should pay heed to them all if he is to understand what he is studying. Most present-day folklorists would reject Tylor's basic concept of the 'meaningless survival' which can only be explained by reference to a remote past; if a belief or custom had really lost all 'meaning', if it did not fulfil some need or give some pleasure, it would not have survived at all. The nineteenth-century folklorists are now blamed for not paying more attention to what functions folklore fulfilled in contemporary society; such functions, even if inarticulately expressed, and even if of fairly recent origin, were at least accessible to direct observation, whereas theories about origins could only be speculations based on chains of alleged parallels.

The new stress on function and context has necessitated changes in classifying and interpreting data. Suppose, for instance, that an informant says: 'My father used to tell me that the old stone goes down to the river to drink when it hears the church clock strike midnight.' This seems very like a survival of primitive animism, and invites speculations about cults linked to prehistoric megaliths. But if the informant adds: 'It was years before I spotted the catch', the father's remark is set in context and is revealed to be a leg-pull, a test of the child's intelligence that turns on the crucial words '. . . when it hears . . .'. The modern folklorist, while not denying that animistic beliefs must have been common in pre-Christian Europe, classifies this item according to its present function as a joke and test, rather than focussing attention on its presumed origin.

A more important application of this distinction concerns the problem of the 'vegetation spirits' and 'corn spirits' to which Frazer, following the German scholar Wilhelm Mannhardt, devoted much attention, seeing them as prime

examples of the survival of archaic beliefs. The corn-spirit is a supernatural being envisaged as an animal or as an old hag, which is frequently mentioned in the folklore of most countries; it is said to lurk in cornfields guarding the growing crops, until captured and killed by the harvesters. Frazer and Mann-hardt were only interested in this belief in so far as it preserved archaic concepts; more recently, however, the Swedish scholar C. W. von Sydow has pointed out that the corn-spirit could and did fulfil a necessary social function which did not entail serious belief at all:

When the last sheaf is often identified by the folk with the wolf, bull, witch etc. that is used to scare children from trampling down the corn, there is nothing mythical in this identification and it does not contain a trace of demonic belief. . . . All these bogy figures that the folk scare children with . . . are purely fictitious beings that the adults only pretend exist, but do not believe in themselves.

C. W. von Sydow, 'The Mannhardtian

Above. A boulder with prehistoric 'cup-and-ring' patterns, at Loch Hakel, Sutherland, Scotland.

Left. A nineteenth-century corn dolly from the Balkans, made of oats and dressed in a silk skirt with ribbons and lace. These dolls represented the corn-spirit in human form; for an example of an animal 'dolly' see Chapter Eight p. 140. Horniman Museum, London.

Theories about the Last Sheaf and Fertility Demons from a Modern Critical Point of View', in *Selected Papers on Folklore*, ed. L. Bödker, Copenhagen, 1948, p. 101.

A further difficulty is that historical evidence for folk customs in the Middle Ages and Renaissance periods is errati-cally distributed and often ambiguously worded or incomplete, so it may be impossible to decide whether, say, a festival briefly alluded to in a medieval source is or is not the same as one well attested 500 years later. The ascertain-able history of seemingly ancient cus-toms can sometimes turn out to be

disconcertingly brief. Thus, the English Jack-in-the-Green, thoroughly studied by Roy Judge in 1979, cannot be traced further back than the late eighteenth century, when it appears in the context of a May Day begging custom of urban chimney-sweeps; its assumed links with older May Day customs are a plausible speculation, but not a provable fact. In seeking our 'window on the past', we should resist the temptation to claim immemorial antiquity for every detail in the picture.

In view of these difficulties, the purely anthropological approach which domi-nated folklore studies a hundred years ago has been abandoned. The only recent scholars using similar assump-tions are certain Marxists such as Vladimir Propp, who, in his *The Historical Roots of the Wonder Tale* (1946), argued that fairytales preserve traces of the social organization of pre-agricultural communities, such as exog-amous marriage and matrilineal in-heritance; he also held that the basic plot-patterns of Wonder· Tales (i.e. fairytales) are derived from archaic initiation rituals and mythical accounts

vant gyfles voit que
faire li conuient. fi re
uient arriere la ou les
pee eftoit fi la prent & la recome
ce a regarder & a plaindre mlt
durement & dift tot en plozant.

of the journey of the dead to the Otherworld.

Insights into the Past

There do, however, appear to be some occasions when material gathered by folklorists can be validly used to help in interpreting the physical evidence supplied by archaeology in order to obtain insights into prehistory, provided it is remembered that folklore can only offer suggestions, not proof, across such wide gaps of time. One example concerns the prehistoric 'cup-marks', pocked hollows found on rocks in parts of Britain, Scandinavia and Northern Europe, whose function and symbolism are unknown. Among the Balts of Lithuania and Latvia, whose conversion to Christianity came late in the fourteenth century, and who preserved many old customs and beliefs to the end of the nineteenth, such stones were still significant even in modern times. The archaeologist Marija Gimbutas, writing in 1963, notes: 'To drill a round hole into a stone was to fecundate the earth force which resides in the stone. Rainwater falling into the hole acquired magic properties. Until quite recently Baltic women coming home from work would stop by such stones to cure their aches and pains by washing in the water.' In Scandinavia and in Scotland, there are records of offerings 'for the fairies' being laid in cup-marks on suitably horizontal surfaces. Such uses cannot be the whole story, since many prehistoric cup-marks are on steep or vertical rock-faces, and could not hold either rainwater or offerings; nevertheless, even if they are only secondary developments, they enrich our vision of the past.

Another striking example concerns the functions of isolated standing stones. Viewing them from the point in time of our own cultural traditions, we might suggest various plausible uses—as memorials, boundary markers, assembly points, symbols of kingship, phallic symbols, and possibly (some now argue) as astronomical devices. But a Jesuit missionary working in Lithuania in 1605 observed something different from all these: 'Huge stones with flat surfaces were called goddesses; such stones were covered with straw and venerated as protectors of crops and animals.' This information is reinforced by the existence of the statue-menhirs of Brittany, or the one on Guernsey which is nicknamed *La Gran'mère du Chimquière* ('Graveyard Granny'), which are roughly carved into a human form with face and breasts; it suggests that even stones without any anthropomorphic features could have been envisaged as persons and 'dressed' accordingly.

Another type of 'window on the past' is offered by early medieval literature. It is generally accepted that most early poems, sagas and romances derive much of their subject-matter from orally transmitted tales, and that in some cases one can recover from these literary sources the outlines of ancient heroic and mythical figures, and of pre-Christian supernatural themes. For over a century there has been much research—and much argument—on how far the Continental Arthurian romances are indebted to oral Celtic sources, and in particular whether their supernatural marvels are based on Celtic mythological material, transmitted from Wales by way of Cornwall and Brittany to the Breton poets employed in French courtly circles. As early Irish literature is far more abundant than that of early Wales, scholars have also explored the parallels between Irish and Arthurian themes; in any case, as Rachel Bromwich has recently written:

It is now becoming generally and increasingly recognised that we

Left. An arm rises from the magic Otherworld beneath a lake to take back Excalibur from the dying Arthur. British Library, London.

Right. In Celtic lore, a severed head is often held to have magic power; it can speak or prophesy, protect or curse, or reunite itself with its trunk. This scene shows the 'Beheading Game' between Sir Gawain and the Green Knight. The latter has allowed Gawain to cut his head off, but remains unaffected; Gawain must, in return, let the Green Knight cut off *his* head a year later. British Library, London.

should think far more in terms of a common fund of narrative themes which were once freely shared among all the Celtic peoples and moved about freely among them, to be appropriated to different heroes as local and national interests dictated – to King Conchobar mac Nessa, Cú Chulainn, and Finn mac Cumhaill and the heroes who surrounded them in Ireland, but to Arthur and his attendant warriors in Britain.

Rachel Bromwich, 'Celtic Elements in Arthurian Romance', in *The Legend of Arthur in the Middle Ages*, ed. P. B. Grout, R. A. Lodge, C. E. Pickford and E. K. Varty, Ipswich and Totowa, 1983, p. 51.

Read thus, an Arthurian text of the thirteenth or fourteenth centuries can illuminate our understanding of pre-Roman Celts. A list of archaic mythological and heroic themes which recur in various guises in Arthurian literature would include: cauldrons of plenty and of rebirth (partial parallels to the Grail, though obviously lacking the latter's Christian Eucharistic symbolism); journeys to the Otherworld; quests for magic objects or animals; fairy wives for human heroes; severed heads with magical powers; sword-bridges; magic females guarding lakes or fountains; the Waste Land; the madness of a hero or seer; the love of a warrior for his king's wife; a magician as a king's mentor; tests of fitness for kingship; supernatural shape-changers who test a

hero's courage. Many of these themes will be found again in the broader context of European folklore, for they are by no means exclusively Celtic.

In a book devoted to the mythological aspects of folklore, it will not be necessary to investigate how much factual truth (if any) is embedded in traditions about Arthur, or about any other historical personage who has become a focus for the accretion of legends. Oral history certainly can convey reliable information over several generations, especially when it is transmitted in the relatively stable and memorable medium of verse; our concern, however, will be with the fictitious elaborations, especially those involving supernatural marvels, which transform persons into heroes, villains

or saints that loom larger than life in local or national traditions. These elaborations are often very similar in pattern at different periods and places, and have parallels in pre-Christian and non-Christian cultures. If it is permissible to include the legends of Odysseus, Perseus, or Oedipus among the mythology of ancient Greece, then certain heroes in European tradition deserve similar consideration for the supernatural elements absorbed into their stories.

Saints' legends also consist of a core of historical fact surrounded by elaborations which stress marvels and miracles, but they pose a difficult problem of classification. How far are they the creation of literate clerics, owing their frequent similarities simply to literary imitation of earlier models? In so far as this is their mode of creation and transmission, they are not folklore, but semi-fictional products of educated culture. Or do they draw upon genuine memories of the saint in question, and upon oral accounts of abnormal experiences (e.g. visions and miracles) circulating among ordinary people? If so, they do come within the definition of folk tradition. The section on saints' legends in Chapter Seven (pp. 80-84) can only indicate, in briefest outline, a few aspects of this vast topic.

There is another use of the term 'legend' which the reader will meet many times in the course of this book. It refers to an oral story, generally brief, describing some remarkable event which the teller fully believes once occurred, usually in his own locality and to people of his own community,

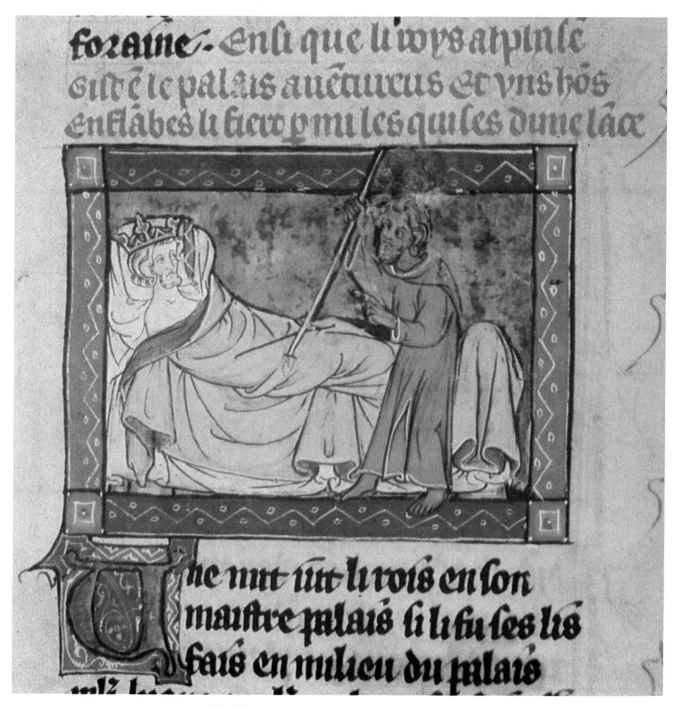

and sometimes even in his own time, or that of his parents. When such anecdotes deal with supernatural topics, such as encounters with ghosts or fairies, or misfortunes caused by witchcraft, they offer by far the most valuable insights available into traditional beliefs. They are not distorted by the prejudices of outside observers, whether these take the form of intellectual or religious hostility, or of sentimental nostalgia. Their value is enhanced by the way the same story-patterns recur again and again, testifying to the tenacity and broad distribution of the concept concerned. This stereotyping did not undermine their credibility to those who transmitted them; indeed, it probably reinforced it, just as two present-day believers in (say) palmistry confirm each other's belief by exchanging strongly similar anecdotes about predictions coming true. Many thousands of such legends have been collected in every country where folklore archives are kept, and many of the standard patterns are demonstrably present already in medieval texts. They are more relevant to our present investigation than 'Wonder Tales' or 'Fairy Tales' of the type collected by the Grimms and others (e.g. 'Snow White', 'Cinderella', etc.), because the latter cannot be taken as indicators of true belief; their magical marvels, their fairies, witches and ogres, are exciting and entertaining fantasies, in a never-never land of once upon a time. It is the folk legend, not the fairytale, which is the best window into the past, and the chief storehouse of European mythology.

The Shaping of the World

Concepts of Creation

A major function of mythology is to explain how the world came into existence, how objects within it acquired their present characteristics, and how social institutions originated. Stories fulfilling these functions are known respectively as creation myths, aetiological legends, and foundation legends (or 'charter myths', in Malinowski's terminology, if their purpose is also to justify the continuance of an institution). In the pre-Christian mythologies of Europe all these can be found, but cosmic creation myths are missing from later folk traditions (except in Finland), no doubt because Christianity insisted upon the Biblical account of God the sole Creator. The Bible was indeed fully accepted, yet alongside it one finds everywhere a profusion of traditional tales claiming that some individual landscape feature was made by someone other than God—usually a giant, giantess or devil, but occasionally a human hero or magician.

Typical are the French legends attributing massive topographical features to the actions of Gargantua, a giant whom Rabelais made famous, but who figured in popular traditions before Rabelais wrote, and has remained popular to this day. It is said that the islands of Mont St Michel and Tombelaine are fistfuls of earth he tossed into the sea; that various rivers were formed where he pissed; that he dug out the bed of Lake Geneva and piled the soil up as Mont Saleve; that certain massive rocks are pebbles dropped from his shoe, quoits that he flung, or remains of food which he sicked up; that various hills are loads of earth which he dropped accidentally while trying to heighten or lower mountains.

Giants were usually thought of as simply stupid and clumsy, but some are malevolent, as in this story collected in Sweden in 1896:

Speaking of trolls and the like, I recall they say that near Svista at Prästberget there had come a giant with a whole boulder on his back. He was on his way to Gamla Uppsala Church in order to destroy it. At Svista he met a shoemaker with a load of old shoes on his back.

'How far is it to Gamla Uppsala?' the giant asked.

'It's incredibly far,' the shoemaker is supposed to have said. 'I'm just coming from there now, and remember, I wore out all these shoes along the way.'

Well, then the giant thought it wasn't worth while to carry that big stone such a long way. He threw it into the field, and it's still there.
John Lindow, *Swedish Legends and Folktales*, London and Berkeley, 1978, p. 85.

It is typical of the internationalism of folktales that an exact parallel to this appears in Charlotte Burne's *The Folk-Lore of Shropshire* (1883-6), telling how the hill called the Wrekin was formed when a Welsh giant was tricked by a cobbler into dropping a spadeful of earth with which he had meant to bury Shrewsbury, with exactly the same lie. Some versions known to Charlotte Burne had the Devil, not a giant, as the hillmaker, a notion which has many parallels. Here, for instance, are a few German accounts of landscape features ascribed to the Devil, all taken from the Grimms' collection of *Deutsche Sagen* (1816):

(1) High in the Rhone Mountains, black basalt cliffs tower above the valley below. When the Devil

*discovered that the inhabitants of the
valley planned to build a church
there, he grew angry and made off
with all the construction stones. He
took them up the cliffs and piled
them on top. No one has ever been
able to get the stones down again.
People say that once the Devil sets a
stone somewhere, no one can move it
again. And even if someone does
manage to cart it away, the Devil will
come and put it right back in place.
(2) Near the church in Cologne one
can see a large stone. It is called
Devil's Rock because imprints of the
claws of the Evil One became
embedded in it when he threw it at
the chapel of the Three Holy Kings.
The Devil was trying to destroy it,
but the attempt failed.
(3) Near the city of Osnabrück an
ancient rock protrudes thirteen feet
out of the earth. The farmers call it
Süntel Rock and say that the Devil
carried it through the air and dropped
it there. They can also point to the
place where the Devil attached a
chain to haul it.*
Donald Ward, ed. and transl., *The
German Legends of the Brothers
Grimm*, London and New York,
1981, Vol. I, pp. 174-5.

It is generally accepted that the motif of
the supernatural rock-thrower and hill-
builder originally belonged to the figure
of the giant, but was increasingly
transferred to the Devil in the course of
the Middle Ages, though the process
was never completely applied. Serious
belief in giants had faded out early,
whereas the Devil was a vivid, living
concept; moreover, the Church preferred to link the sites of alleged
supernatural events to Christian figures,
whether saints or demons.

Some landscape legends depict a
conflict of good and evil creators. In
Iceland, it was said that Satan grew
angry when God made the sun, and
tried to extinguish it by pissing at it; he
only succeeded in making Mývatn Lake.
Similarly, German peasants explained
certain rock formations near Weissen-
berg with the following story:

*The Devil wanted some land of his
own, and he requested some from the
Lord God, who agreed on the
following terms. The Devil would
receive as much land as he could
enclose between walls before
cockcrow. The Evil One set to work
at once, but just as he was about to
set the final stone and complete the*
*wall, the cock crowed. Furious that
his hopes had been dashed, he tore
down his own structure in rage and
scattered the stones in all directions.
The ruins are still said to be haunted
by spirits.*
Ibid., p. 172.

Such stories are now only told light-
heartedly, but it is possible to discern
deeper reasons why there should have
been interest in the idea of secondary
creator-figures whose actions were at
best foolish, and often deliberately
hostile to humanity. A significant factor
in these legends is that they always
relate to the unproductive features
of a region—stony land, deep ravines,
rocky mountains, awkward boulders

Left. Merlin building Stonehenge. A fourteenth-century illustration to Layamon's poem *Brut*, which followed Geoffrey of Monmouth's *History* (c. 1147) in saying that Merlin brought the stones from Ireland and set them up on Salisbury Plain. British Library, London.

Right. This huge monolith in Rudston churchyard, North Yorkshire, is traditionally said to have been hurled by the Devil in the hope of smashing the church; as usual, he missed his target.

intruding into agricultural land – not to pastures, arable land, productive woods. Peasant communities, it seems, readily accepted that good land was made by God for the use of mankind, but felt that anything useless and inconvenient to themselves needed a different explanation, which the Bible did not supply. Nor would they have agreed that wild scenery was 'good' in the sense of 'beautiful'; the taste for picturesque wilderness only developed late in the eighteenth century, among the educated classes. Medieval aesthetics were different; beauty then consisted of orderliness, and the ideal was that all nature should be cultivated and made fruitful. Rugged landscapes, like the wildness of animals, were regarded by most theologians as a result of Adam's sin. As late as 1684, Thomas Burnett argued, in his *Sacred Theory of Earth*, that God must have made the earth as a smooth ball, on which mountains only appeared when it was smashed out of shape by the Deluge, in punishment for sin. Folktales ascribing unwelcome landscape features to sec-

ondary creators were seeking to transfer responsibility for these blemishes from God to an evil or stupid being.. Also, such tales always show the Devil (or giant) being foiled in his schemes, or failing through clumsiness; the implied message is: 'That rock is ugly and useless, but it was the Devil, not God, who put it there, and at least it did us less harm than he intended.'

When useful features of a landscape are ascribed to a sub-creator, he naturally will be a benevolent personage, usually a saint. There are innumerable such stories, and they are not limited to Catholic areas. Springs well up where a saint strikes the ground, or where his horse paws it, or where his blood is shed, and their waters have healing powers. Holy trees grow where a saint's staff takes root. In medieval Wales, writes Elissa Henken, local saints were the Christianized form of the folk hero:

Amongst their other roles, they are also culture heroes, helping to create and define the world, as geomorphic constructors – making wells, raising hills, changing the course of rivers, confining the sea – and as benefactors, providing man with both physical and cultural necessities – food, healing, law. . . . The saints provide fruitful land, turning swamps, sea marsh and rocky land into good arable land, and ensuring the proper amount of rain.
Elissa R. Henken, 'The Saint as Folk Hero: Biographical Patterning in Welsh Hagiography', in *Celtic Folklore and Christianity*, ed. Patrick K. Ford, Santa Barbara, 1983, pp. 58, 70.

Occasionally one encounters benevolent sub-creators who are not saints but figures surviving from pre-Christian mythologies. A pseudo-historical Irish work from the twelfth century, *The Book of the Conquest of Ireland*, describes groups of early settlers who are probably rationalized memories of pagan deities; they cleared vast plains, dug lakes, and instituted many crafts and customs. Finnish traditions are more explicitly mythological, and they concern the whole earth, not just certain

features of it. The *Kalevala* tells how the great hero Väinämöinen (or, in some versions, his mother Luonnotar) was floating in the primordial ocean when a waterfowl mistook his (or her) raised knee for a tussock, built a nest on it, and laid a gold egg. The hero jerked his knee, and the egg fell and smashed in the water:

*From the cracked egg's lower
   fragment
Now the solid earth was fashioned;
From the cracked egg's upper
   fragment
Rose the lofty arch of heaven;
From the yolk, the upper portion,
Now appeared the sun's bright lustre;
From the white, the upper portion,
Rose the moon that shines so
   brightly;
Whatso in the egg was mottled
Now became the stars in heaven;
Whatso in the egg was blackish
In the air as cloudlets floated.*
W. F. Kirby, transl., *Kalevala: The Land of Heroes*, Everyman edition, London, 1907, vol. I, p. 7.)

Another curious creation myth is a Lettish or Latvian legend which seems to blend Christianity with echoes of two Scandinavian myths, one about the gods dismembering a primeval giant, and the other about a mighty eagle whose wing-beats cause all the winds of the world:

At creation God sent forth his word as a gust of wind, which bore an eagle. He made darkness and light, and banished the eagle to the former.

The bird rebelled, and was dismembered by God. His blood became the sea, his body mud, and from the two halves of an egg within him came heaven and hell. Inside these were a white sticky mass and a black sticky mass, which became angels and devils, and within the lower shell mud collected, forming the earth.
Venetia Newall, *An Egg at Easter*, London, 1971, pp. 29-30.

Christian influence on these stories is obvious, and there has been considerable argument as to how much archaic material they contain. The bird seeking a nesting site in the *Kalevala* resembles both Noah's dove and the Holy Spirit 'brooding like a dove' over the waters in *Genesis*; in many versions Väinämöinen turns the broken egg into the cosmos by the power of his word, like Jehovah. The Lettish story also echoes *Genesis*, and perhaps shows traces of Manichean heresy by asserting that the material universe came from the remains of an evil being. Nevertheless, there are so many non-Christian parallels to the concept of creation from an egg that the Finnish and Lettish tales are best seen as fusions of Christian and archaic themes.

Recently, Professor Carlo Ginzburg has drawn attention to a strange statement made by a miller called Menocchio while he was being interrogated on suspicion of heresy, in northern Italy in 1584. This man would not accept that God had made the world out of nothing. Instead, he held that a

formless chaos existed already, 'and out of that bulk a mass formed—just as cheese is made out of milk—and worms appeared in it, and these were the angels.' One witness alleged that Menocchio had once said, even more startlingly, that the world had 'curdled like cheese' when 'thrashed by the water of the sea like foam', and that the worms in it 'became men, of whom the most powerful and wisest was God.' It is clear from many passages in his statements that Menocchio's outlook was predominantly rationalistic; here, he seems to be trying to explain the development of the universe in materialistic terms, using an assumption, scientifically quite acceptable at his period, that living creatures can form in decaying or fermenting substances by 'spontaneous generation'. There is, however, a very ancient Indian myth that the gods made this universe by 'churning' a primordial sea till it coagulated. This myth might have spread westwards; nineteenth century ethnologists recorded that the Kalmuks of the Altas Mountains held that in the beginning the sea formed a 'skin', like that on milk, from which plants, animals and men emerged. Ginzburg claims that this tradition had persisted orally for some 2,000 years in the peasant sub-culture, reaching Menocchio by this 'underground' route. It may be so; on the other hand, cheese-making and the apparently spontaneous appearance of maggots are universal phenomena, which widely separated cultures and individuals can seize upon independently and spontaneously as a familiar analogy when trying to explain the unknown processes of creation more-or-less realistically.

Concepts of the Cosmos
Besides creation, mythology and folklore are concerned with the way the universe is structured. According to one archaic belief, reflected in folklore, it is envisaged as having three zones or levels (sky, earth, underworld), linked by a solid vertical axis passing through the centres of all three; this axis is described as a World Pillar, a World Tree, or a World Mountain formed of metal or glass, which is often said to have seven terraces. This cosmology is now only

Left. Strange features, especially large prehistoric structures, might be explained as the work of antediluvian giants. This illustration from a Dutch book of 1660 shows a local gallery grave known as the Giant's Tomb being built by giants and men together.

Right. Huge isolated boulders might be said to be missiles flung by the Devil, a giant, or a hero. This rock is said to have been hurled by the Estonian hero Kalewipoeg at a wolf. Kalewipoeg was of gigantic strength and was always benevolent to men. The traditions about him were collected by F. R. Kreutzwald in the 1850s.

Below. Luonnotar floating on the primeval waters. An illustration to the *Kalevala*.

found in its full form among non-European peoples, notably those of central Asia and the circumpolar regions, but there are signs that some elements of it existed in pre-Christian Europe too. At the time of the conversion of Saxony, for instance, in 772 A.D., Charlemagne ordered the destruction of a sacred pillar called Irminsûl, which the Saxons held to represent the axis of the world. Then there is the well-known Nordic version of the World Tree: the ash Yggdrasil, rising through the centre of Middle Earth, having its roots in the world of the dead, and linked in some way to the world of the gods. The surviving descriptions of it are slightly inconsistent; one poem talks of 'nine worlds in the tree', a more complex picture than that in the Icelandic *Prose Edda*. Whatever the details, there is no doubt of the cosmic importance of Yggdrasil.

Traces of these conceptions appear in fairytales, where they usually have lost all serious impact (no one would claim Jack's Beanstalk as a Cosmic Tree, even though he reaches a world of ogres by climbing it), and function simply as decorative motifs in the magical adventures of heroes. Even so, they can appear quite startlingly archaic when one knows how far-flung and ancient their parallels are. For instance, there is a French fairytale called 'The Green Mountain' which was collected from a storyteller in Brière in 1950, which includes not only an excellent example of a World Mountain but also an allusion to the belief that a magician can

reduce himself to a skeleton, use the bones as a magic ladder, and then reconstitute himself from the bones again – a belief known in Tibet and the East, and in the shamanistic practices of Siberian and Central Asian peoples. Yet the fairytale itself is told purely as entertainment, as is normally the case with stories of this genre. Its hero has been set the task of climbing the Green Mountain, which is 200 feet high and all slippery; he receives this advice from the Devil's daughter, who is acting as his helper:

Here's a stewing-pot I've brought you. You are to fill it with water, make up a good fire in it, and put me to boil in it, bit by bit; you are to take all my bones, remove the flesh, and drive a bone into the side of the Green Mountain to serve as a ladder for you; using all my bones, you'll reach the top. . . . As you come down, you must gather up my bones and put them in a napkin; then you must put them to boil in the stewing-pot, when you have come down again to the foot of the Green Mountain; then I'll come back to life again.
My translation, from Michèle Simonsen, *Le Conte Populaire*, Vendôme, 1984, pp. 106-7.

In Eastern Europe, survivals of old cosmologies are more numerous and significant. The Romanians speak of a Sky Pillar; the Lithuanian account of the

The Giants of Ath, Belgium. Many towns in Belgium, Holland and Northern France keep figures of benevolent giants as civic mascots and parade them on festive occasions. The only surviving English example is at Salisbury.

world of the dead (see below, pp. 38-9) includes both a Cosmic Tree and a Cosmic Mountain; in Greek folk beliefs, goblins called Kalikantsaroi spend most of the year in a deep cavern, trying to saw through the roots of a tree which supports the earth and the sky, but which renews itself faster than they can destroy it. In a Hungarian fairytale, 'The Tree that Reached to the Sky', the hero climbs a tree so tall that it takes him ten days to reach the first branch, which is to him like a whole world, where his further adventures are set.

Hungarian storytellers, even in very recent times, have treated their fairytales more seriously than is common in Western European traditions; scholars who interrogated them in the 1950s found that many fantastic elements in the tales were widely taken to be absolutely true. One famous storyteller, Lajos Ami, told an interviewer that the sky is solid and 'is set down on the rim of the earth like a tent'; at the Creation it had been low and flat, so that 'if someone had had a five-metre ladder he could have got into the upper world where God and Paradise are', but God thrust the sky up higher with his cane, to make more room for birds. There is a door in the sky, through which Adam and Eve were thrown down out of Paradise after sinning. When asked 'Above which country is this gate?', Ami

replied, 'I have no way of answering this. But I know that Adam and Eve fell down between Vienna and Buda, so that's where the gate has to be.'

Medieval Christianity had its own richly symbolical version of the Cosmic Tree, the Legend of the Holy Cross. Briefly summarized, this tells how when Adam was dying his son Seth obtained three seeds of the Tree in the Garden of Eden from the angel guarding its gates, and laid them in Adam's mouth. Adam was buried under a hill at the very centre of the world, and a triple tree sprang

The Holy Thorn at Glastonbury, Somerset, is descended from one said to have grown from the staff of St Joseph of Arimathea, which miraculously sprouted leaves when he stuck it in the ground. It flowers at mid-winter, on or about 6 January, Old Christmas Day.

from the seeds in his skull. The hill was Golgotha, 'Place of the Skull'. The triple tree was felled, and Solomon tried in vain to use its trunk in building the Temple; centuries later, Christ's Cross was made from its wood. Symbolically, the Cross is a new Tree of Life,

stretching from the centre of earth to Heaven, and set on the hill above Adam's grave; Christ dies on the vertical axis of the universe, reconciling all worlds in himself.

Exemplary Punishments

Fusions of Christian teaching and archaic themes occur at a more local level in topographical legends, especially those about places lost under water or sunk underground, and those about sinners turned to stone. These motifs, which predate Christianity, have always been used moralistically. One need only think of Atlantis, drowned because of the pride and ambition of its people; of blasphemous Niobe, turned into a crag from which flows a river of tears; of the Phrygian pool described by Ovid, which submerged a region whose inhabitants (except for Philemon and Baucis), had refused hospitality to gods disguised as beggars. The Bible also has two legends of this type: Lot's wife turned to a pillar of salt for disobedience, and the destruction of Sodom and Gomorrah, whose ruins, later tradition asserted, were covered by the Dead Sea. Thus folktales about drowned villages and petrified sinners could claim Scriptural precedent; they were used to explain the origins of landscape features and, more importantly, as moral warnings.

Many coastal areas have legends about regions submerged by the sea. The Welsh tell of a fertile plain once filling much of Cardigan Bay; early versions say God 'turned the sea over it' because of its ruler's pride, while later ones blame a drunken steward for opening its floodgates. Off Cornwall lies the lost land of Lyonesse, first mentioned by William of Worcester in the fifteenth century. The story probably arose from the observation of ancient stone walls which are visible at low tide off the Scillies, the area having suffered subsidence; legend dramatized the process into one overwhelming flood, from which only one man escaped. In Brittany this story-pattern is very popular, with no fewer than twelve cities allegedly lost to the sea. The best known is Is, whose legend was first recorded in 1637. It was a magnificent city, built on land reclaimed from the sea, but the king's wicked daughter opened the floodgates when going to meet her lover (who in one version is Satan), and the waters rushed in. The king, warned by St Gwendolé, fled on horseback; the girl tried to cling to his horse, but the saint pushed her off and she drowned.

Similar stories are told elsewhere of lakes appearing suddenly to engulf a castle or a whole town, from which only one man escapes; in some Welsh examples the disaster is God's vengeance on a murderer and his descendants, while in others it is heretics who are punished, or simply (at Ellesmere in Shropshire) a woman too miserly to let neighbours draw water from her well.

In mountainous countries, landslides play the same role. The Swiss equivalent to the legend of Philemon and Baucis tells how a rockfall in the Grindewald Valley buried a village where only one poor couple had sheltered a wandering dwarf. A glacier near Berne is said to cover a once fertile farm, whose proud owner used cheeses to build a soft path up the mountain, and lavished dainties on his dog and cow while refusing food to his old mother. Near Innsbrück in the Tyrol, children were warned against wasting bread by being shown Frau Hütt, a towering crag overhanging the valley. They were told that she was a giantess who wickedly wasted bread, 'God's holy gift', by using it to wipe her son's grubby face. At once a thunderstorm broke out, followed by a landslide:

When the skies finally cleared, the fertile fields of grain, the green meadows and forests, even the house of Mother Hütt, had all disappeared. Instead, there was only a desert of scattered stones and cliffs; not even a blade of grass grew there. In the midst of all this desolation stood Mother Hütt. She had been turned to stone, and there she will stand till Judgement Day.
Donald Ward, vol. I, p. 198.

In folk tradition, turning to stone is commonly a punishment for dancing in impious circumstances – on Sundays or

Left. A modern rendering of the Old Norse world-picture. Yggdrasil, the Cosmic Tree, holds within its branches Middle Earth with its encircling sea, the outer ring of rocks where giants live, and the rainbow overhead. Supernatural animals are in its branches and roots; the great Sea Serpent encircles the earth.

Right. Plant designs are popular in the folk art of eastern Europe, possibly recalling the Cosmic Tree. This Hungarian horn box of the nineteenth century was used by a shepherd for carrying veterinary ointments. Néprajzi Múzeum, Budapest.

Below. A Lappish shaman's drum from northern Sweden, c. 1800, used in magic rituals. The figures represent creatures of the Otherworld, and at the top is a triangular shape flanked by stars which may be the Cosmic Mountain. Staatliche Museum für Völkerkunde, Munich.

holy days, inside churches, or while a religious procession is passing. Playing sports or working in the fields on Sundays can draw the same fate. Stories about this are attached to several groups of standing stones in the south of England and in northern France, including the Merry Maidens in Cornwall, the Noce de Pierre at Pont-Aven in Finistère, and the Stanton Drew circles in Somerset. Modern commentators sometimes suggest that such legends may preserve memories of prehistoric rituals involving dancing at these sites, but there is no real need to postulate this; medieval clergy constantly denounced dancing as a sensual pleasure leading to sin, and condemned still more any dancing in a holy place or on a holy day. Protestant clergy were even more severe on the point. The likeliest explanation for these legends is that they developed from a famous medieval *exemplum* against dancing (i.e., a story for use in sermons), and became attached to prehistoric stones through the natural urge of storytellers to 'prove' their story by pointing out some impressive object allegedly connected with it. In any case, the tale of the petrified Sabbath-breakers is told about natural rocks too, not exclusively about megaliths.

The *exemplum* in question, 'The Dancers of Kolbeck', is first recorded in 1075, and purports to be a true account of a miracle in a German village in 1012.

Sixteen peasants held a dance on Christmas Eve instead of attending Mass, and would not stop when rebuked by the priest, who cursed them: 'May God and St Magnus force you to dance for a whole year!' So they did, despite rain and frost, heat, hunger and thirst, and although they danced ceaselessly their shoes never wore out. When one girl's father tried to drag her away, her arm broke off, but still she danced. At the end of the year the Bishop of Cologne freed them from the curse. Four dropped dead; the rest wandered through Europe as beggars, telling the story wherever they went.

In this, the earliest version, there is no link to any topographical feature, but as the story spread such links were often added, in order to 'prove' it and to fit it to a new local setting. In Sweden, where it is known as 'The Harga Dance', it is said that the dancers were led out of their village, Harga, by 'a well dressed gentleman with horse's hooves for feet' who took them up onto a mountain peak, where they danced until only their skulls were left, and a circular groove had been worn into the rocks. Modern attempts to find this groove, the existence of which might have inspired the localization of the tale, have failed.

In Iceland the story is attached to Hrúni, where there is a depression in the ground resembling the shape of a church. Long ago, it is said, there was a priest there who used to hold a dance inside his church for his parishioners on Christmas Eve, 'with drinking and gambling and other unseemly sports going on far into the night'. As a result, one year 'church and churchyard sank into the earth, with all the people inside it, and onlookers heard shrieking and howling from deep underground.' A new church was built further down the valley, but no one ever danced in it on Christmas Eve.

Above. Callannish Stones, Isle of Lewis, Outer Hebrides. These are said to have been giants turned to stone by St Kiaran, because they met in council to reject the Christian faith he was preaching.

Above right. The bread-and-cheese ceremony at St Briavels, Gloucestershire. Originally the food was thrown to the people inside the church itself, from a raised gallery, but this was thought irreverent, and it is now thrown from the churchyard wall.

Just-So Stories

Origin stories can be told also about characteristics of animals and plants, in the manner imitated by Kipling in his *Just So Stories*. Here too Christian influence is marked, the stories being usually linked to Christ or the Virgin, to Old Testament episodes, or to saints. However, there certainly were earlier tales of this type involving pagan deities; classical examples include the myths about Echo and Narcissus, Minerva and Arachne, Apollo and Hyacinthus, which set out to explain the characteristics of echoes, narcissi, spiders and hyacinths. Medieval and post-medieval European examples are so numerous that it is enough to summarize a few widespread ones which are typical of the genre:

The dog's nose is cold because Noah used it to stop up a hole in the Ark.
The aspen trembles because its wood was used for the Cross.
Spiders bring luck because one spun its web across a cave entrance to conceal Mary and the infant Christ from Herod's soldiers.
The weeping willow droops because its twigs were used to whip Christ.
The donkey has a cross on its back because it carried Christ to Jerusalem.

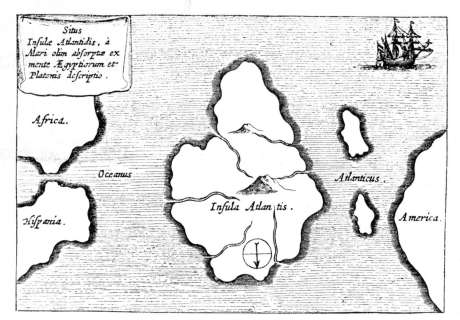

The ones about birds are particularly picturesque. In Czechoslovakia they say the cuckoo was a woman who hid when Christ passed her house lest he should ask her for bread; when he had gone by she poked her head from a window, crying 'Guckuck!' ('Look, look!'), and was turned into a cuckoo. In Norway, it is the woodpecker who was a woman too mean to give Christ a decent-sized bannock or cake, so he cursed her: 'You shall become a bird and seek your food between bark and bole, and never get a drop to drink when it rains.' In France, Germany and Estonia the woodpecker is doomed to peck thirstily at trees because at Creation it refused to join other birds in helping God to dig wells in the ground. In the Tyrol, they say ravens were white, till the Christ Child cursed them for fouling his drinking water.

Creating the world also involves making mankind, and establishing ethnic or occupational sub-groups in society. The Bible account of the creation of Adam and Eve seems to have been found satisfactory; one of the few folkloric elaborations upon it comes from the Hungarian story-teller Lajos Ámi, who said they were hairy all over at first, but through eating berries from a magic plant soon after leaving Eden they lost all hair except on their heads, armpits, and pubic region. This legend, however, is characteristic of the Near East and Asia, not of Europe.

Tales about the origins of ethnic groups are of particular interest for implying social attitudes, whether of pride in identity or of inter-group hostility. Thus, Norwegians allege that Lapps do not descend from Adam but from a lump of horse dung to which Christ gave life, or from the copulation of Cain with a bitch–in other words, Lapps are not fully human. There are many stories about Gypsies, some told by themselves, some by outsiders. Some say they are doomed to wander because they are descended from Cain, or because a Gypsy smith forged nails for Christ's crucifixion; others counter-claim that he made the nails small and thin, so the Virgin Mary gratefully blessed all Gypsies, saying their work would be light and their profits good. Another legend, expressing Gypsy pride, explains that the first time God made a man he burnt him in the oven, thus creating a Negro; the second man he undercooked, producing a pallid white man; the third, just pleasantly browned, was the first Gypsy.

One curious legend, 'The Hidden Children of Eve', has been put to several uses. It has served to explain the origin of fairies, and thus to imply kinship between them and humans (see p. 49); to account for social classes; even, in south-east Europe, to explain the origin of apes. One version, given by Philip Melancthon in a letter in 1539, can be summarized thus:

It was a feast day, and Eve was washing her children. Looking out of the window she saw God coming. As she had not finished washing them all, she hid the unwashed ones away. When the children were presented to the visitor, he began questioning them on their knowledge of the Creed. Abel, Seth and the sisters managed all right, but the hidden ones, including Cain, could not recite it. Consequently, Abel was marked out to be a priest, Seth a king, and Cain and the hidden ones to be serfs.

Reider Th. Christiansen, 'Some Notes on the Fairies and the Fairy Faith', in *Hereditas*, ed. Bo Almquist, Breandán mac Aodha, and Gearóid mac Eoin, Dublin, 1975, p. 99.

Here, a creation legend becomes what Malinowski dubbed a 'charter myth', not merely explaining the origin of class distinctions but claiming divine authority for their continuance. Folklore is full of small pseudo-historical 'charter myths', i.e., legends that authorize a custom or enhance the prestige of a group by referring back to some venerated figure of the past. Thus, English blacksmiths claimed superiority over all other trades by saying King Alfred had granted it to them after a blacksmiths' strike reduced the kingdom to helpless confusion. Upper-class families often claimed that their aristocratic status, and/or their tenure of specified lands and privileges, came as a reward to some ancestor for killing a dragon or other monster. In Scotland,

the Somervilles, who were barons of Linton and bore a dragon on their crest, said the Barony had been created in 1174 for a John Somerville who slew a dragon. In County Durham, the Conyers family, who held the Manor of Sockburn from the Bishop of Durham, did so on condition that they showed each new Bishop at his installation 'the falchion wherewith the champion Conyers slew the worm'.

Again, at St Briavels in Gloucestershire, it is said that some long-gone Earl of Hereford granted the villagers in perpetuity the right to cut wood in a certain coppice, his wife having wrung the concession from him by riding round the coppice naked; the event is commemorated by an annual distribution of bread and cheese at the church. It all seems trivial now, but in previous centuries the right to gather wood was of considerable economic value to the poor, and was put at risk when common land was enclosed as private property; the appeal to the memory of the heroically charitable Countess was an attempt to counteract the cold legalism of landowners and lawyers.

Such foundation legends were naturally presented, and accepted, as historically true; even today, despite the scepticism of trained historians, a vivid story linking a custom to the communal or national past is normally welcomed and believed by the group whose activities it glamorizes. A remote origin seems almost a guarantee of stability; whether the point at issue is the status of blacksmiths or the shaping of a landscape, folklore, like religion, cherishes the formula '. . . as it was in the beginning, is now, and ever shall be, world without end, amen.'

Fairylands and the Realms of the Dead

Otherworlds in mythologies and in folk beliefs are of two kinds: one for non-human beings of various types, and one for the human dead. Often they are described as distant realms, but almost as frequently they are imagined to lie so close alongside normal space that transition from one to the other is only too easy, in both directions. Certain places and times facilitate the transition. Supernatural powers break through into the normal world (or can be summoned to it) at turning-points of time: midnight, midday, New Year's Eve, Halloween, May Eve, Midsummer Night. Similarly with space; it is at boundaries, thresholds, crossroads, fords, bridges, and where verticality intersects the horizontal, as on top of mounds, down wells, under trees, that Otherworlds are accessible. As Alwyn and Brinley Rees wrote in *Celtic Heritage* (1961):

To the questions 'Where is the Other World', 'Is it one or many?', the answers furnished by myth are contradictory. It is the 'lower' half of Ireland, the land under the earth or the síd*-mounds. It is also 'the land under the wave', an island, or a whole series of islands beyond the sea. Yet it can manifest itself in other places. A mist falls on us in the open plain, and lo, we are witnessing its wonders. . . . The limits of such a world cannot be defined in terms of distance or direction. Situated far beyond the horizon, it is the goal of the most perilous journey in the world; present unseen all around us, it can break in upon us 'in the twinkling of an eye'.*
Alwyn and Brinley Rees, *Celtic Heritage*, London, 1961, pp. 342–3.

One key is ambiguity, the concept of both/and and neither/nor. If a man stands exactly on the boundary where three parishes meet, on the stroke of midnight, in which parish is he, and what date is it? He has cut loose from normal space and time. He has also reversed normal human conduct by going outside at night, the time when supernatural beings are active, but humans should be asleep. In such circumstances, he places himself in contact with 'the other'; he can reach, or be reached by, fairies, ghosts or demons.

Voyages to Fairyland

Let us begin, however, by considering Otherworlds 'situated far beyond the horizon', only to be found by exceptional heroes after exceptional efforts. A type particularly well represented in Celtic lore is the Otherworld across or beneath the sea, usually to the west or north. The theme was a favourite in medieval Ireland, where famous literary renderings include *The Voyage of Bran Son of Febal*, *The Voyage of Maeldúin*, and the *Navigatio Sancti Brendani*. Clerics approved of these tales and preserved them, seeing the quest for the Otherworld as analogous to the soul's journey towards Heaven, the Promised Land. Some of the wondrous islands seen by Maeldúin are obviously allegories; the Isle of Women is a warning against lust, the Isle of the Ancient Eagle a symbol of spiritual renewal. But *The Voyage of Bran* is not Christianized in this way. Its hero is seeking a magic region with 'thrice fifty islands full of women and sweet music', where sickness and sorrow are unknown. There is also another blissful land, down on the seabed, which Bran has passed without even realizing it exists; Manannan, one of the pre-Christian Celtic gods,

Above. A knight embarks for the Island of Love. This scene from a late medieval love allegory draws on the old theme of magic voyages to the Otherworld. Österreichische Nationalbibiliothek, Vienna.

appears to him and tells him:

Along the top of a wood
Your coracle has sailed, over ridges;
There is a wood of beautiful fruit
Under the prow of your little skiff.

In *The Voyage of Maeldúin*, the seafarers reach one place in the Atlantic where the water is transparent, like thin cloud, and they can peer down on to a lovely country with groves, mansions, and herds of grazing cattle. This belief in a world on the floor of the ocean has persisted in Irish tradition to modern times. Its inhabitants were not imagined as mermaids, but as beings in human form, whose way of life paralleled human society; stories were told about fishermen bringing up in their nets such homely objects as a sprig of heather, a cooking-pot full of potatoes, or even, occasionally, a child of the underwater people, whom they wisely released at once.

There are also Irish and Welsh traditions about islands that magically appear and disappear—traditions no doubt confirmed by the occasional occurrence of mirages. Off the coasts of Connemara, it is said, the fairy island of O'Brasil rises out of the sea once every seven years, on the verge of the horizon; if someone could reach it before it sinks and throw fire onto it, it would be fixed forever. Such legends may have been one factor encouraging westward voyages of exploration.

Norwegian traditions are virtually identical. There too there is an underwater land, Utrost—so called because it lies beyond Rost, the furthest real offshore island. At times it rises so near the surface that fishermen see corn poking up above the waves, and find barley in the bellies of fish. Men whose boats are sinking are sometimes saved, if they deserve it, by Utrost rising suddenly under their keel. Legend tells of one man saved in this way, to whom the inhabitants of Utrost showed their pastures and cornfields before leading him safely home; they gave him food, tobacco, and magic fishhooks which brought him good catches ever afterwards.

Inland, there can be watery Otherworlds in lakes and rivers. This theme appears as a romantic motif in Arthurian literature, notably in connection with Lancelot, whose cognomen 'du Lac' refers to the underwater fairyland where he grew up. But when Gervase of Tilbury, in the thirteenth century, describes how people at Arles fear beings in the Rhône whom they call Dracs, he is not talking of a literary motif but of a living belief:

These Dracs, they say, have their abode in caverns under rivers, and occasionally, floating along the surface in the form of gold rings or cups, they entice women or boys who are bathing by the river banks, for as they try to grasp what they see, they are suddenly seized and dragged down to the bottom. . . . Sometimes, after they have spent seven years there, they return to our hemisphere. These women say they lived with the Dracs and their wives, in ample palaces in caverns and the banks of rivers.

Quoted in K. M. Briggs, *The Vanishing People: A Study of Traditional Fairy Beliefs*, London, 1978, p. 73.

Gervase himself had spoken to one woman who claimed to have been kidnapped and held captive by Dracs.

Fairy Hills

As for Otherworlds located underground, every country in Europe has stories about mountains, hills or mounds which house supernatural beings, by whatever names these are locally known (elves, dwarfs, trolls, earthmen, fairies, etc.). Unlike the vanishing islands, these hills and mounds are real places, generally close at hand; however, their magical status is often guarded by taboos which set them aside from common use—it may, for instance, be thought unlucky to plough them or let cattle graze them. These taboos, incidentally, have saved many ancient burial mounds and earthworks from destruction, to the delight of archaeologists. Even in modern times there remains, in some regions, a reluctance to intrude on the Otherworld; on 23 April 1959 the *Daily Mail* reported that a road being built in County Mayo had to be rerouted, because workmen refused to destroy a 'fairy palace' which was in the way, fearing this would bring disaster.

The fairy world inside mounds and mountains is usually pictured as full of riches, merriment and feasting, but dangerous to mortals who enter. They may be held captive, or attacked and killed. In Denmark there was a tradition that on certain nights hillocks under which trolls lived rose up on gold pillars, and one could watch the trolls feasting. In many countries there are stories claiming that some fine cup or drinking horn belonging to a local family or to a church, had been stolen from a fairy mound. A typical one, from Sweden, begins:

There was a hill in Ljungby where the trolls lived. The coachman of the estate was daring enough to ride there. When he got there, the top of the hill was lifted up, and they were dancing under it. Then one of them came out and offered him something to drink. He took the horn and rode off. But he happened to spill a few drops on the horse, and it burned the skin right off.
John Lindow, p. 102.

Mountainous regions have stories about mining dwarfs, and also about vast treasure-filled caverns which someone glimpses once, but can never find again, as in this German legend about a place called Untersberg, 'Wonder Mountain':

On one occasion a master woodsman was caught on the mountain by darkness and had to spend the night in a cave. In the morning he came upon a cliff from which heavy, glittering gold sand was flowing. . . . He saw a door open into the cliff. He looked inside, and the scene was as natural as if he was looking into a special world inside the mountain that had daylight just as we have. However, the door only remained open a moment, and when it slammed shut, the inside of the mountain reverberated like the inside of a great empty wine barrel. . . . Since then, no one has ever seen the door in the cliff again.
Donald Ward, vol. I, p. 153.

Time in the Otherworld is not like human time. The Irish hero Bran spent one year, so he thought, in the Isle of

Women, and then longed to see his home again. The fairy women warned him that though he could indeed *see* Ireland, he must stay in his boat and not set foot on shore; he obeyed, but one of his companions did not, and as soon as his foot touched land he crumbled into dust, for centuries of earthly time had passed since Bran and his men went to the Islands, and by rights they should have died long ago. This eerie notion recurs in Welsh and Scottish folktales.

Blissful fairylands can also act as refuges for the human dead or for those 'Sleeping Heroes' suspended between life and death (see pages 70, 72). The most famous example is of course Avalon. In his *Vita Merlini* Geoffrey of Monmouth wrote that Arthur went, gravely wounded, to an 'Island of Apples' or 'Fortunate Isle':

It needs no farmers to plough the fields. There is no cultivation of the land at all beyond what is nature's work. It produces crops in abundance, and grapes without help, and apple trees spring up from the short grass in its wood. All plants, not merely grass, grow there spontaneously, and men live a hundred years or more.

This island, Geoffrey says, is ruled by nine sisters, the eldest and wisest being Morgan, who undertook to heal Arthur of his wounds. He does not say that the dead go there, but the blending of fairyland with a land of the dead is fairly frequent in folklore. A Breton ballad, 'Le Frère de Lait', describes an island of the dead which is full of apple trees; the dead drink from its clear streams to renew their strength, and then live there joyfully singing and laughing.

Sometimes the two types of Otherworld are completely assimilated. A medieval English poem, 'King Orfeo' (probably based on a lost Breton lay), turns Orpheus's visit to Hades into a visit to fairyland. Pluto is a king of the fairies, who kidnapped Euridice as she slept under an apple tree at noon; his kingdom is beautiful and his palace gorgeous, but Orfeo sees grim, mutilated human ghosts mingling with the fairies there. Similarly, a nineteenth-century Irish tale tells how a man joined a merry band of fairies going to a fair on Halloween; as he danced with them his eyes were opened, and he saw that 'all the dancers, men, women and girls, were the dead, in their long, white shrouds.'

Journeys of the Soul

The World of the Dead is a complex concept, blending Biblical imagery, medieval Catholic doctrines, and some non-Christian elements. The latter are naturally strongest among peoples whose conversion came late, notably the Balts of Latvia, Lithuania and Old Prussia. They held that at death a man's being splits into three components: the

body, and two forms of spirit. One, the *siela*, is reincarnated as a tree, a bird, or a baby in the same family as the dead man; the other, the *vélé*, sets out on a long journey to an Otherworld beyond the sky. It may ride through the air on horseback, fly in bird form, rise in the smoke of the pyre, or go by boat, as the sun was thought to do. On arrival, it has to climb a sheer stony hill, using animal claws or its own long fingernails, to meet God. Then it must go further yet, to a remote place where stands a great iron post, or a tree with silver leaves, copper branches, and iron roots – it may be a birch, oak, or apple tree. This is the World Axis, where the *vélés* will live in the branches, visited nightly by the sun. On the anniversary of their deaths, and during the October Feast of the Dead, the *vélés* return on horseback to visit their families. As late as the seventeenth century, Latvians would lay the skin and guts of a horse on a grave, to help the return of the dead.

Nowhere else is the scenario so consistent, but its components can be parallelled singly in other cultures. Reincarnation as a tree, for instance, is the main motif of an international fairytale which the Grimms called 'The Juniper Tree'. It is also implied by a common folksong cliché about plants springing from the graves of separated lovers, as in a version of 'Earl Brand':

The one was buried in Mary's kirk,
* The other in Mary's quire;*
The one sprung up a bonny bush,
* And the other a bonny briar.*

These twa grew, and these twa threw,
* Till they came to the top;*
And when they couldna farther gae,
* They cast the lovers' knot.*

The description of the Latvian spirit-world reflects the old cosmologies discussed in the last chapter. The methods of reaching it find parallels in Viking Age Scandinavia, where boats or horses were frequently burned or buried with corpses, and where it was held that a man's spirit rose up in the smoke of his pyre. Standing stones from the eleventh century in Gotland (Sweden) bear carvings of ships and riders that probably represent the journey of the dead. The annual return of the dead is powerfully described in an Icelandic poem of the tenth or eleventh century, *The Lay of Helgi Hundingsbani*. The dead Helgi returns from Valhalla to his burial mound, where his wife meets him and makes love with him once more; at dawn he bids her farewell:

It's time I rode the red sky-paths,
* They redden now towards day;*
It's time I made my pale horse run
* Along the steep sky-way.*

Across the bridge of the windswept sky
I must go the west,
Before the cock at the world's end
* Wakes warriors from their rest.*

A famous Scottish ballad about the return of the dead, *The Wife of Usher's Well*, has an enigmatic reference to an Otherworld tree:

It fell about the Martinmass
  When nights are lang and mirk,
The carlin wife's three sons came
  home,
  And their hats were o' the birk.

It neither grew in syke nor ditch,
  Nor yet in any sheugh,
But at the gates o' Paradise
  That birk grew fair eneugh.

The long, painful journey of the dead also featured prominently in Christian thought. There is a whole series of medieval texts, dating mainly from the seventh to the thirteenth centuries, containing visions of the afterlife allegedly seen by men in trances. The visionaries describe roads leading through Hell and Purgatory to Heaven, full of hideous ordeals; their macabre imagery made a strong impression on popular piety, though they have not been adopted into official Catholic doctrine. Thus, one seer spoke of a broad iron bridge over a river of flaming pitch; the virtuous crossed easily, but when sinners stepped onto it it became as narrow as a thread, tossing them into the pitch, from which they crawled back to try again, and again, until at last, 'burned and purged of their sins', they could cross over into Heaven. Thurkill, an Essex farmer who had a trance in 1206, saw a long bridge studded with spikes, leading from Purgatory to Heaven; along it souls slowly crawled, bleeding in every limb. Others describe ladders; these were a favourite image in sermons and religious art, for they could symbolize the laborious attainment of virtue as well as the journey of the dead, and had a Scriptural precedent in Jacob's ladder.

Perhaps the strangest vision is that of Gottschalk, a German peasant, in 1189. Lying sick, he fell into a five-day trance, in which he was led by angels through the realms of the dead. The first thing he saw was an unusually large linden tree, every branch laden with shoes; beyond stretched a wide wasteland, overgrown with piercing thorns. The souls of the dead flocked there; those who had shown charity in life took shoes from the tree, but the rest went barefoot, in great agony. Beyond the thorny plain another torture awaited them – a river filled with swordblades.

These medieval images reappear in the well-known *Lyke Wake Dirge*, from northern England in the sixteenth century; it tells how the dead must cross Whinny Muir ('Gorse Moor') and the Bridge of Dread to reach Purgatory fire, and how shoes given away in charity can be used against the thorns, which otherwise will 'prick you to the bare bone'. A contemporary commentator remarks contemptuously that women would sing the dirge when keeping watch by a corpse, and that they seriously believed it wise to give new shoes to a poor man once in their own lives, because after death they would have to cross barefoot 'a great launde full of thornes and furzen', unless an old man met them there with the very shoes they had once given.

Another grim folk-belief drawn from medieval Catholicism is the spectral death-cart of nineteenth-century Brittany, which comes at night to fetch the dying. It is drawn by skeletal horses, and driven by the Ankou, a personified Death who appears as a tall, gaunt man, or as a skeleton with a scythe. It was generally said that the last person in a parish to die each year must act as the Ankou for the whole subsequent year. This way of personifying Death certainly derives from late medieval art; his cart may owe something to memories of the corpse-laden carts used during plagues. Some said the Ankou was taking the dead to a realm across the seas; others, to the churchyard; others, to a pit in the Bois de Huëlgoat which was an entrance into Hell.

As this shows, the world of the dead need not lie far away; like fairy Otherworlds, it may be set in the local landscape. Etna, Vesuvius, and the Icelandic volcano Hekla have all been reputed to be mouths of Hell or of Purgatory. Ireland has its Patrick's Purgatory on an island in Lough Derg, famous since the twelfth century as a place where those who keep vigil may experience a foretaste of the tortures of the afterlife, to expiate their sins; it is

still a popular centre for a penitential pilgrimage encouraged by Church authorities.

European countries, both Catholic and Protestant, are full of stories about wretched ghosts undergoing their punishments here on earth, in the places where they sinned. Some early medieval theologians, e.g. Gregory the Great and Hugh of St Victor, believed in expiations of this type, but the notion was soon officially discarded in favour of an 'otherworldly' conception of Purgatory. Folklore, however, has preserved the concept of earthbound penitential ghosts. Some labour in vain to make ropes of sand; some carry heavy boundary stones, having cheated neighbours of their land; women guilty of abortion or infanticide wash bloody linen forever; misers wander till they

can tell someone where they hid their money; criminals haunt the site of the gallows, and suicides their unhallowed graves; unbaptized babies cannot rest until someone, deliberately or accidentally, gives them a name. Such legends proliferate everywhere; they may not fit well with orthodox doctrines about the afterlife, but they express and reinforce, in a highly dramatic way, society's condemnation of various offences against the moral code.

Often the tormented ghost is that of some locally notorious personage. One instance must suffice here, that of Lady Howard of Tavistock in Devon (1596-1671), who married four times and is commonly but wrongly supposed to have murdered all her husbands:

Every night, it is said, Lady Howard sets out from the old gatehouse [of Fitzford House, her home], in a carriage of bones adorned at the four corners with the skulls of her four husbands, and drawn by headless horses. In front of this nasty equipage runs a black dog with a single eye in the middle of its forehead. All proceed round the old road skirting Dartmoor till they reach Okehampton Castle, another of her seats. She alights there and picks one blade of grass from the castle mound, returns to her carriage, and back to Tavistock. All this must be repeated until the mound is bare.
Theo Brown, *The Fate of the Dead: Folk Eschatology in the West Country after the Reformation*, Ipswich and Totowa, 1979, p. 32.

One particularly interesting motif is the Wild Hunt, widespread in Scandinavia, Germany, the Low Countries and northern France, and also occurring sporadically in Britain and Ireland. It has two sub-types, often overlapping. In one, the Hunter is a solitary ghost, doomed to hunt for ever because in life he had broken the Sabbath for love of the sport, or had trampled the crops of the poor. In the other, he is a demonic figure who rides through the air leading a host of damned souls, with spectral horses and hounds, and sometimes devils too. The Wild Hunt is particularly associated with midwinter nights (Norwegians call it *jolerei*, 'the Christmas Host'), but may appear at other seasons too. It is sometimes said

Among the macabre images popular in late medieval art is that of Death driving a cartload of corpses. Detail from Breughel's *The Triumph of Death* (c. 1562). Museo del Prado, Madrid.

Not gnomes, but real miners, whose leather working clothes and peaked caps were the model for traditional depictions of underground dwarfs. Illustration from Georgius Agricola, *De Re Metallica* (1556).

to emerge from inside a mountain, e.g. at Hörselberg in Thuringia. Its coming is heralded by fearful noises–thunder, roaring winds, the howls of demonic dogs–and it flattens everything in its path. The sinful ghosts are mutilated and deformed, and cruelly tormented by the accompanying demons and dogs. Anyone who sees the Wild Hunt approaching should fling himself face down with his arms spread like a cross, lest he be swept up to join them.

Various rationalizations have been suggested to explain this belief: whirl-winds, the cries of migratory birds passing by night, hallucinations. Such factors certainly are relevant to the persistence of the belief, though whether they are its sole origin is more doubtful. On the other hand, many scholars, from Jacob Grimm onwards, have linked it with Indo-European gods, particularly the Germanic Wotan/Odin and the Hindu Rudra. A few areas of Jutland and southern Sweden do indeed name the Hunter Odin, while in Austria and Bavaria the Hunt is led by a female figure, Perchta, who is probably derived from a Germanic goddess. In most regions, however, the Hunter remains anonymous, and in those where he is given a name it is likelier to be that of a legendary human hero or of a historical personage than that of a deity: Sigurd and Gudrun in Norway, King Valdemar in Denmark, Charlemagne, Dietrich von Bern or Frederick the Great in Germany; most frequently of all, it is a local landowner or cleric reputed to have led an evil life. The supernatural roots of the belief probably should not be sought in the cult of one particular

god, but in more general notions such as survived in the Baltic cultures, where all the dead were said to ride back to earth through the stormy skies of late autumn.

One category of the dead whose fate aroused special anxiety is men drowned at sea. If their bodies are not found they will become particularly fearsome ghosts, resenting their lack of burial. If, however, their bodies are washed ashore and buried, there was a fear that the sea, cheated of its due, would drown someone else or flood the land. A Jutland legend tells how people once charitably buried a drowned stranger's corpse in the village churchyard. That night, a gale arose, and for three days and nights it blew sand over their fields, threatening to ruin them forever. The villagers consulted a wise man, who told them to reopen the grave; if the body had not stirred, all was well, but if it had started sucking its forefinger that meant it was not human but a merman, and must be reburied on the beach below highwater mark. This was done; the storm ceased; and Jutlanders never again buried unknown corpses in hallowed ground. (The sucking of the finger, incidentally, alludes to a widespread belief that vampires and other evil 'undead' chew their shrouds and their own limbs.)

In Scotland, too, bodies washed ashore were sometimes buried where found, below the tidemark; otherwise, says a Hebridean proverb, 'the sea will search the four russet divisions of the universe to find the graves of her children.' But in south Sweden the stress is on the necessity for Christian burial;

The interior of the West Kennet Long Barrow, Wiltshire – a massive structure to serve as a house for the dead. Even centuries of Christianity could not entirely root out the instinctive idea that the dead are somehow present in their graves.

the unburied would become 'strand-ghosts' haunting beaches and nearby houses, screaming 'Help us to hallowed ground!' Their bodies must be found and brought to a churchyard or, if that proved impossible, the beach itself and the offshore waters must be blessed by a priest.

Norwegian lore told what happens if a drowned man's body is never found. He turns into a *draug*, a squat, powerful creature whose face is tangled seaweed, and whose voice is a blood-curdling shriek; he is seen or heard when gales are brewing, and his presence is an omen of death. On Christmas Eve *draugs* may come ashore; anyone meeting them will go mad, unless (as happened, legend asserts, on Luröy Island in 1837) he summons the Christian dead from the churchyard to drive these unhallowed beings back into the sea.

This Norwegian sea-*draug* takes his name from Old Norse *draugr*, the word for a corpse which 'lives on' in the grave, from which it may emerge as a physically violent ghost – an ancient, simple, and very widespread notion of what, and where, the realm of the dead

is. Medieval Icelandic sagas, though written in Christian times, contain many stories on this theme; they do not idealize the world inside the grave-mound, describing it as a gloomy chamber where the dead man sits guarding the weapons buried with him. The *draugr* will attack anyone who digs into the mound, and may also roam the countryside, breaking the backs of cattle, horses and men. He must be overcome by wrestling, and then laid by decapitation and burning. Similar tales circulated in twelfth-century England, possibly introduced by Vikings; William of Newburgh's *History of the Kings of England* includes four allegedly true accounts of corpses leaving their graves to attack people. When exhumed, they seemed to be undecayed, so they were burnt to ashes. At Castle Alnwick, the suspected corpse looked bloated and red-faced, so some men hit

it with a spade, 'and immediately there gushed out such a stream of warm red gore that they realised that this blood-sucker had battened on the blood of many poor folk.' This detail evidently implies belief in vampirism of the type so notorious in Greek and Balkan folklore; its occurrence in England is puzzling, for Norse *draugar* do not suck blood, nor does the motif reappear in British lore until reintroduced through literary channels in the nineteenth century.

The Benevolent Dead

The dead who live on in their graves need not be always envisaged as hostile to the living; many, on the contrary, are benevolent influences. The Lithuanians, whose concept of the double soul was discussed above, also held that the dead man remained alive in his grave; if he had been given food, drink and tobacco

A cemetery at Agkhazic, Georgia, USSR, in 1986; on one grave stands a table holding fruit and wine. There is a Greek and Russian Orthodox custom of placing food on tombstones on major festivals or on the anniversary of death, in accordance with the Biblical injunction: 'Lay out thy bread and thy wine on the grave of a just man' (Apocrypha, *Book of Tobias*, 4:18). The custom was also known in parts of Western Europe in the late Middle Ages; Rabelais alludes to it in France in his own time.

at his funeral, and if feasts were held at his graveside on Church festivals, he would give prosperity to his family and farm. In Norwegian folklore the *haug-bonde*, 'mound-dweller', was regarded as the guardian of the farmstead and as the ghost of its first owner; some nearby

hillock would be assumed to be his grave, and offerings of milk, ale or poultry would be made there. Grad-ually, however, the *haugbonde* was thought of less as a ghost and more as a type of household guardian fairy, like British Brownies. The same thing happened in the Orkneys, where a creature known as a *hogboon* ap-parently began as a ghost inhabiting a burial mound, as his name shows (from Old Norse *haugbúi*, 'mound dweller'), but by the nineteenth century had evolved into a helpful, but occasionally teasing, fairy of the Brownie type. Once again, the fairy world and the world of the dead turn out to be connected, not opposites; the evolution from ancestral ghost to fairy has probably occurred in many cultures, and is one (though only one) of the roots of the belief in elves, fairies, and related beings, which is the topic of the next chapter.

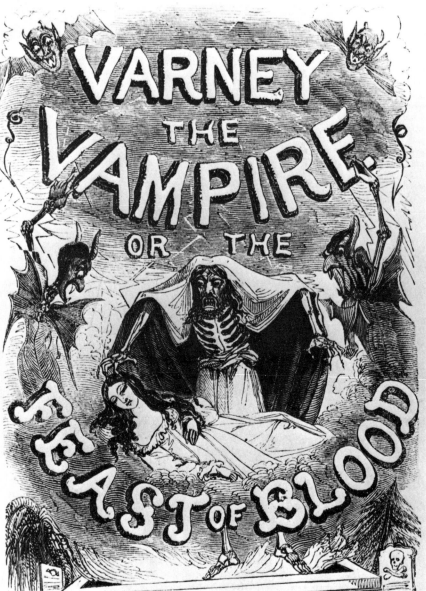

Above. A group of Christmas mummers dressed as 'Frightful Perchtas'; Salzburg, Austria. Wearing fearsome masks and rattling chains and bells, they impersonate the demonic midwinter spirits; for their benevolent counterparts, see Chapter Eight, p. 125.

Left. Fear of vampires was particularly acute in the late eighteenth century in Eastern Europe. Their reputation was spread in the West through literary works such as *The Vampyr* (1819) by Byron's friend Polidori; they became a favourite topic for writers of 'Penny Dreadfuls' such as this one, of 1847.

Fairies and their Kin

The Fear of Fairies

It is hard for us to grasp the role which belief in fairies played in rural communities before the coming of mechanization, education, and modern medicine. The romanticism of nineteenth-century writers and painters, the daintiness of children's books, the commercialism of the tourist trade, have combined to reduce fairies, pixies, brownies, leprecauns and dwarfs to silly clichés throughout most of Western Europe. But 200 years ago there was almost universal belief among the peasantry in a race (or several races) of non-human but material beings. They were visible or invisible at will; they could fly, change shape, cast spells; they were very long lived, perhaps immortal; they lived underground, in water, and in woods. Sometimes they were friendly, giving prosperity or teaching useful skills; on the other hand, they could inflict disease, steal babies, and abduct people. The clergy usually insisted that such beings could only be demons, but in popular culture they were fitted into the Christian world-picture in ways which preserved their moral ambiguity. One common legend identified them as 'the hidden children of Eve' (see p. 32), thus making them remote kinsmen of mankind. Another said that they had been angels who, when Lucifer rebelled against God, were uncertain which side to join; they were cast out of Heaven, but, not being wicked enough for Hell, remained wherever they fell—on earth, in the sea, in the sky.

In parts of Eastern Europe this belief-system is still operative, as can be seen from fieldwork done by Gail Kligman in Romania in 1975-6:

The rusalii *or* iele *are mythical fairies who are generally believed to be white-clad maidens of extraordinary beauty. They are three, nine, seven or eleven in number. . . . They are members of the supernatural order, implicitly a sacred one, and they must be treated accordingly. Hence, a linguistic taboo applies to the very name of these mythical beings. . . . The categorical term for these female spirits is* iele, *the third person plural feminine pronoun . . . [which] literally means 'they' as opposed to 'we'. . . .*

Thus, we see that the iele *live in water, whether a lake, swamp, marsh, spring, or at the edge of one. Otherwise, they inhabit forests, crossroads, hillocks, mounds, fields, or places which have not been explored by human feet. In general,* iele *are thought to be found in non-cultivated areas, areas that are not civilized by humans, areas outside the village. Unlike people,* iele *travel at night, dancing and singing. They may or may not be accompanied by a bagpiper. A circle left where they dance (the grass having been burned under them) remains barren. Their dances are so fast and complicated that it seems they do not even touch the ground. . . .*

They are usually considered to be pernicious beings. Their limited benevolence is manifested in connexion with music or occasionally with healing. . . . However, their kindness is overshadowed by their malevolence. If anyone breaks an interdiction, even unintentionally, the fairies strike. One is said to be 'taken' or 'possessed'. . . . They paralyze or disfigure offenders. 'They make you deaf, crippled, blind; they may even murder.' 'They make you crazy.'. . . . Anyone entering their dance will be 'hit'; whoever listens to their incomparably beautiful singing will be left deaf; whoever answers the fairies when they call will remain mute and/or deaf for life. . . . Their most typical victims are young men; it is thought that the iele *try to steal their masculine strength. . . .*

The iele *are believed to be most dangerous during Rusalii [Whitsuntide]. . . . However, many claim the fairies are very active throughout spring and summer, or that they can be harmful at any time of the year. . . . Their power is concentrated between midnight and dawn, until the rooster crows.*
Gail Kligman, *Căluş: Symbolic Transformation in Roumanian Ritual,*
Chicago, 1981, pp. 49-51.

Though this account is so recent, every detail in it can be matched repeatedly in records from earlier centuries throughout Europe; its grim picture of ruthless beings inflicting human sicknesses exemplifies one major theme in traditional fairy lore. Noteworthy, too, is the evasive name *iele*, 'They'; everywhere, fairy names are either euphemisms (Good People, Good Neighbours), generalized descriptions (Little People, Hidden Folk, Underground Ones, Wood Women), nicknames based on appearance (Jenny Greenteeth, Redcap), abbreviations of human names (Nisse from Nicolas), or old and seemingly meaningless words whose roots only scholars would recognize (Puck, Pixie, Troll, Elf, Nix, Boggart, Bogy). 'Fairy' itself is derived, through medieval French, from Latin *fata*, 'the Fates'. Behind all these circumlocutions lie fear and unease aroused by dangerous supernatural powers.

Fairies were 'mythical', but the troubles they were blamed for were real enough. They included cramps, stitches, sudden dizziness and blackouts, rheumatic pains, heart attacks, heatstroke, sunstroke, oppressive nightmares. Some tales about a human being entering fairyland end grimly, saying that he or she returned half crazed, and died soon after; this may be based on the experiences of amnesiacs, or of stroke victims. In Scotland and Ireland various cattle diseases were blamed on 'elf-shot', i.e. flint arrows or sharp slivers of wood flung by fairies at their victims; these also caused rheumatic pains in human joints. Horses found tired and sweating in their stalls were said to be 'fairy-ridden' or 'hag-ridden.'

The worst deed ascribed to fairies was stealing a baby and substituting a changeling—an ugly, fretful creature, always sickly and hungry, which was really one of themselves. This belief has been held for centuries; about 1215, Jacques de Vitry defined a *chamium* (from Latin *cambiatus*, 'changed') as ' a child who exhausts the milk of several wet-nurses, but to no avail, for it does not grow, and its stomach remains hard and distended.' Various congenital abnormalities, mental defects, and deficiency diseases were thus conveniently accounted for; it was perhaps less distressing to parents to feel they were persecuted by fairies than to wonder whether God was punishing them for a sin. The belief also encouraged good standards of childcare, since it was held that fairies could not steal a baby unless it was alone. Unfortunately there was a darker side; once a changeling had been identified as such, tradition recommended that it should be maltreated, for instance by beating or burning it or leaving it on a dunghill, in hope that its fairy mother would hear it screaming and remove it, returning the stolen baby instead. There is a widespread tale about how a changeling was startled into betraying its true nature, and then re-exchanged in this way; interestingly, present-day Irish versions omit the traditional burning or beating, stressing instead that one must treat a changeling kindly, so that the fairies will be equally kind to the kidnapped baby.

Guardians of House and Farm

The relations of fairies to humans can be classified along a sliding scale from benevolence to malevolence, and (partially corresponding to this) a scale from intimacy to remoteness. At the 'friendliest' end of both scales is the 'house-spirit': English Brownie, German Cobold, Russian Domovoy, Scandinavian Nisse or Tomte, etc. As a rule, there is only one on each farmstead, and he embodies the luck of the place; in return for small offerings of bread and milk or porridge he works by night at

domestic and agricultural tasks. As the Grimms wrote:

In some villages every peasant, along with his wife, sons and daughters, has a Cobold who performs all sorts of domestic chores. He carries water into the kitchen, chops wood, fetches beer from the cellar, cooks, brushes the horses in the stable, clears the manure out of the stalls, and the like. Where the Cobold is present, the cattle increase in number, and the whole farm is successful and prospers. Even today, when a maidservant accomplishes her tasks with despatch, the proverb is cited, 'She has a Cobold!' But whoever vexes the Cobold had better take care!
Donald Ward, vol. I, pp. 68-9.

Medieval Germans sometimes displayed figurines by the hearth, which they identified with their Cobolds; these could be of wood or wax or cloth, about two feet long, and were sometimes kept in boxes. Alternatively, the Cobold might be imagined as a child-sized goblin, or rather like a cat. There was a famous one called Hinzelmann (from *Hinze*, a cat's name), who allegedly inhabited a castle near Lüneburg in the 1580s; oral stories about his helpful deeds and comic pranks formed the basis for a chapbook and various later written accounts, which spread his fame.

Polish and Russian lore describes a whole group of household spirits with specialized spheres. The chief one is the Domovoy (from *dom*, 'house'), who lives behind the stove or under the threshold; others inhabit and protect the cellars, barns, stables, sauna, yard, and chicken-run. The Domovoy should be respectfully addressed as 'grandfather'; he brings luck, works secretly in

51

the farm, and gives death warnings by groaning or wailing. People moving house used to carry hot embers from the old stove to the new to induce the Domovoy to follow, and put out bread and salt to welcome him. Such small food offerings are a feature of the cult of house-spirits at all periods, from the Roman Lares and Penates onwards. No doubt the food did disappear–taken by mice or cats or hedgehogs.

It was often thought that the luck a house-spirit brought to his farm was 'stolen' from some neighbour's, and that if annoyed he would reverse the process, as in one common Norwegian anecdote: One day, a wealthy farmer saw his Tusse puffing and groaning as he dragged a single barley ear towards his barn. 'Why are you puffing like that? It's not much of a load,' said he. 'If I take as much away as I'm bringing, you'll soon see what the load is,' answered the Tusse, as he turned and dragged the ear towards a neighbour's farm, which had never done well. The farmer's eyes were opened, and he saw the single ear was really a huge stack. From that day, nothing went right for

Anyone who enters a fairy ring to join in their dance will disappear into fairyland for years, or forever. Illustration to a Welsh legend in Wyrt Sykes, *British Goblins* (1880).

him, but his neighbour flourished.

A house-spirit should never be laughed at, spied on, or cheated of his due, or he will revenge himself. Another Norwegian legend, recorded in many variants, tells how a servant girl envied the good creamy porridge she had been told to put out for the Nisse at Christmas, so she ate it herself, and put out a trough of coarse meal and sour milk. The Nisse 'rushed out and grabbed her and started to dance with her. He kept it up until she lay on the ground gasping for breath, and when people came out to the barn in the morning she was more dead than alive.' An English story from nineteenth-century Sussex tells of a farmer who

spied on fairies at work, and laughed on hearing one say to another 'I say, Puck, I sweats; do you sweat?' The fairies rushed at him in anger, striking him hard on the head so that he fell unconscious; a year later he died, 'sorry enough that he'd ever interfered with things that didn't concern him.'

An odder taboo, associated with house-spirits everywhere, and with them only, is that they run away if given clothes. Many stories offer no explanation; those that do, are inconsistent. A few say that the fairy took offence because the clothes were of poor quality; others that he grew too conceited to work. In an Irish version, a Púca declares: 'I can't work in these fine clothes. I must be off to town to let people see what a fine gentleman I am.'

House-spirits were also thought to be sometimes noisy and mischievous, like poltergeists. A sixteenth-century English account of 'Hobgoblins or Robin Goodfellows' says that they take up their abode in houses, 'making in them sundry noises, rumours, mockeries, gawds and jests, without doing any harm at all,' and that people get so

Any small, mysterious object might be thought to belong to fairies. Prehistoric flint arrows were said to be weapons with which they inflicted diseases on men or cattle; in some districts fossilized sea urchins were called 'fairy loaves' because they look like buns. Royal Pavilion, Art Gallery and Museums, Brighton.

used to them that they are not frightened. French Lutins and Italian Monacielli behave similarly, breaking crockery, pulling bedclothes off, hiding things, and making odd noises. They were regarded as irritating, but not alarming.

There are other types of fairy which do not live in houses but visit them by night to see if they are well kept. Such are the Sicilian 'ladies from outside', who roam from house to house on Thursday nights, blessing those that are tidy and clean and where food and drink have been left out for them. Where they find slovenliness or disrepect they will inflict poverty and sickness, unless quickly appeased. Sicilian peasants still took the belief seriously in the 1950s; its value in promoting hygiene is evident.

Out of doors, other guardian fairies each had their sphere of action. Some protected hedgerow and garden trees, notably hawthorn (in Ireland) and elder (in Scandinavia and England); no branch should be cut from such trees. In Latvia and Lithuania, dwarfs under the roots of elder-bushes were as vital to the luck of the farm as house-spirits were

elsewhere. Equally important were the grotesque 'field guardians' and 'corn spirits' common throughout all Europe. Whether male, female, or animal-like, they punished anybody who harmed growing crops, and were described as horrifying bogies. The Austrian and German 'Corn Wives' were hags with long, black, iron breasts, who sucked the blood of children who picked wild flowers in cornfields; the Russian Poleviki, who grew taller as the crops grew, used sickles to slash drunkards who trampled the plants; the Italian Pavaró, dog-headed and with iron teeth and claws, protected bean fields; the goat-spirits of Germany, Yugoslavia and Scandinavia, hid among the corn

and charged intruders.

Certain Slavonic field-spirits, notably the Russian Poludnica, were particularly dangerous at midday – one of the critical turning-points of time, and one which, according to Psalm 91, was haunted by demonic spirits inflicting sickness. The Poludnica was a danger to anyone who works in the fields during the heat of the day:

In Posexon'e, Jaroslav Province, people know of a special spirit 'poludnica': a beautiful, tall girl clad entirely in white. In the summer, during the time of harvest, she walks in patches of rye, and she takes by the head those who work at noon, and begins to turn it, until she has worked it into burning pain. . . .

It is for this reason that people must not work at noon. . . . By the way, people do not believe this now [i.e. c. 1910] and regard these stories as old wives' tales.

Quoted by Felix Oinas, 'Poludnica, the Russian Midday Spirit', *International Folklore Review* 2, 1982, p. 133.

Iris, by J. A. Grimshaw (1886). A Victorian conception of a fairy; the insect wings are a 'literary' invention, but the erotic charm and the lonely woodland setting correspond well to genuine folk tradition, e.g. the Rusalka or the Fata Padourii. City of Leeds Art Gallery.

How far, and for how long, such beings were seriously believed in has been much debated (see p. 15), but undeniably they have ended their careers as bogies for scaring children and keeping them well away from growing crops.

Water Spirits

Much the same is true of the next category, water-dwelling fairies, whose appearance and behaviour reflect the characteristics of their habitat, while also deterring children, and others, from going near dangerous places. They are described in vivid terms, and fall into three groups: grotesque ogres and ogresses; seductive but dangerous maidens; and shape-changers who shift between human form and that of an animal, generally a horse.

Slavonic lore is rich in water-spirits. The male ogre type is the Vodanoy, which haunts any inland water, running or stagnant, and particularly millponds; he will drag down swimmers and drown them, and eat their flesh. The Vodanoy

was described in many guises: a huge half-human frog; an old green-haired man; a floating log; a giant; or, in Bohemia, a clump of pretty water-weeds tempting children to lean too far over the water. He was said to hibernate under the winter ice; then in spring he would awake in fury, and would create devastating floods unless appeased by offerings such as a pig or horse.

The females, the Rusalka, are said to be the wives of the Vodaniye, and also, in some areas, to be ghosts of women who drowned themselves. Those of North Russia look like pale corpses, with glowing green eyes; further south, especially in the Danube valley, they are beautiful but dangerous, because their sweet singing lures young men into the rivers, where they drown. Rusalka alternate between land and water; in winter they stay under water, appearing occasionally as the weather warms, and at Whitsun go ashore into the woods. In summer they are tree-fairies, sitting in the branches and dancing in clearings. It

used to be customary to hang rags on their trees, to honour them. Both Vodaniye and Rusalka evidently symbolize aspects of the seasonal cycle.

In France, Germany and the Celtic countries, legends about water-fairies are less concerned with their role as nature-spirits than with their sexual attraction, and with unions between them and humans. All end sadly, when the man breaks some taboo laid on him by the fairy, losing both her and the luck she had brought him. A Welsh story tells how a man married the fairy of lake Llyn y Fan Fach; she warned him never to strike her, and when he did so, though lightly and playfully, she vanished into the lake. But her three children remained, and they and their descendants became skilled doctors, because she had taught them herb lore. In France, a famous fourteenth-century legend tells how Count Raymond de Lusignan married Melusine, a water-fairy, but spied on her in her bath and saw how her legs turned into snakes.

Left. A Domovoy; drawing by I. Bilibine, 1934. This Russian house-spirit looked like a little old man, his body covered in soft fur; like many other house-spirits, he may be identified with the soul of the first owner of the house he protects.

Right. A shoemaker and his wife watch as their helpful goblins find the new clothes set out for them; illustration by George Cruikshank for an English translation of Grimm's *Fairytales*.

Below. A Polevik; drawing by I. Bilibine, 1934. This Russian corn-spirit guarded the growing crops by making intruders dizzy or strangling them. He had a mud-coloured body, hair like grass, and eyes of different colours.

She fled, shrieking; from then on she would be heard shrieking, like an Irish banshee, whenever a Lusignan was about to die. In England, instead of romantic tales like those, one finds a female bogy-figure used by parents to scare children away from deep pools and wells; she is a cannibal witch called Jenny Greenteeth, known chiefly in Lancashire and Cheshire, and she is associated—or even identified—with a type of small weed which forms a carpet over stagnant water.

Shape-changing water-spirits, generally horses or bulls, were common in northern Germany, Scandinavia, and in Scotland, where they are called Kelpies. The story most often told about them is that they appear on land near rivers or lakes, looking just like ordinary horses, and seeming so tame that tired travellers are tempted to mount them; all at once, the horse rushes into the water, drowning its rider. A popular Danish variant tells how six out of seven boys mounted an unknown horse, whose

A Rusalka in a tree; drawing by I. Bilibine, 1934. Like other female nature-spirits, the Rusalka's power lay in her erotic attraction; she lured men into the forests or the lakes, and killed them there.

back grew longer and longer to accommodate them. The seventh exclaimed, 'By Lord Jesus' cross, I've never seen a longer horse!', at which the fiendish creature bolted into a river, drowning the six. Scottish Kelpies behave similarly, and also are dangerous to girls, whom they seduce while in human form, and then drown.

Fairies of Wild Places

Such beliefs and legends carry warnings of the dangers of the unfamiliar—it is the unknown horse, the young stranger, who may be a Kelpie in disguise. In proportion as the peasant moved further from his home ground, the supernatural creatures he expected to

meet grew more menacing. There might be will-o-the-wisps flitting over marshes to mislead and drown him; these were sometimes explained as ghosts (especially of unbaptized babies), and sometimes as small elves with lanterns.

Various goblins haunted lanes and waste ground on the outskirts of villages, frightening travellers at night by appearing in grotesque forms and uttering weird sounds. Of these, some, like the French Lutins and Fadets and the English Pixies, operated in groups. Others were solitary, and associated with one particular spot; many fanciful names were given them (in English, Barguest, Shuck, Kow, Gytrash, etc.), and they were often said to appear as

dogs, horses or calves, generally headless or with fiery eyes. Sometimes the helpful house-spirit and the mischievous outdoor goblin share the same name, e.g. Irish Púca or English Puck. The latter name, as we saw above, was applied to Brownies in Sussex, but Shakespeare's Puck is a typical teasing shape-changer:

I'll lead you about, around,
Through bog, through bush, through
*   brake, through briar;*
Sometime a horse I'll be, sometimes
*   a hound,*
A hog, a headless bear, sometime
*   a fire.*

Fairies are universally credited with this

power of making people lose their way by tricking them with lights, imitating human voices, or casting bewildering spells to make paths and landmarks unrecognisable. In densely cultivated countries like Britain, the belief has dwindled into light-hearted stories such as are told about Cornish Pixies and the Welsh Pwca. It is a different matter among mountains or in deep forests, where losing one's way might mean death. This fear finds expression in legends about tree spirits, and the rules which must be observed so as not to annoy them. In Russian and Czech lore, it is said that men who enter forests to hunt, pick mushrooms or chop wood, must keep to the paths and not go far

among the trees, otherwise an angry Leshy–a huge figure with blue skin, green eyes, green hair and beard–will lure or panic them into going further and further in, till they are lost and exhausted. Curiously, all over Europe the counterspell against all 'pixy-leading' fairies is the same: one must remove clothes and shoes, turn the clothes inside out, and put the shoes on the wrong foot.

Despite dangers, many people had work which took them into mountains and forests: huntsmen, charcoal burners, herdsmen, shepherds. Legends about encounters with supernatural beings were common among them, and still occur in some regions, for instance

in the mountains of north-western Romania, where the following accounts were collected in 1972:

Most often, Fata Padourii is seen by shepherds during their night watch. The wind usually rises, the sheep become afraid, and then she appears. Frequently she has the face of a lovely girl. One old man claimed that when he saw her she was wearing only an embroidered Hungarian blouse. He called out to her, but she would not answer, and when he gave chase and was almost to her, she turned into a tree. When another shepherd chased the beautiful girl, she dissolved into a wisp of smoke, and

for another she simply vanished before his eyes. Another man, returning from a difficult trek through the woods on a cold winter night, was confronted with 'a mountain of snow' at the edge of the village. It had no substance when he touched it, but there was no way he could pass. Suddenly it vanished, and he knew it was Fata Padourii. All those who have seen her agree that she cannot speak, though she often wails like the wind, and sometimes sings when she is in the form of a girl.
David Summers, 'Living Legends in Romania', *Folklore* 83, 1972, pp. 326-7.

There is an element of erotic fantasy here which is common in traditions about the fairies of wild places. In Swedish lore, a female forest spirit, the Skogsra, gives a hunter good luck by blowing on his gun, or keeps watch by a sleeping charcoal burner's fire; in return, she expects him to make love with her. The front of her body is beautiful, but her back is like a hollow tree; when the man discovers this, he flees. In Norwegian tales, trolls and she-trolls make amorous advances to dairymaids and herdsmen tending cattle on the upland summer pastures; they should be driven off with gunfire, certain herbs, or the sign of the cross. Legends about these erotic encounters always imply disapproval of them.

Men working underground, particularly in metal mining, encountered fairies of a different sort: the dwarfish 'mine-spirits', known in English lore as Knockers, and elsewhere as Earth-Mannikins, Dwarfs, etc. The relationship was rather like that between farmers and their Cobolds; the Dwarfs guided the miners to good lodes by their knockings, or warned them of dangers, in return for small food offerings. They could also be mischievous, and would punish those who offended them. In seafaring lands such as Denmark and the Low Countries, there was a corresponding belief in small luck-bringing spirits inhabiting their ships, who would help the captain in times of danger. In these concepts, there was no element of fear; the psychological functions of belief in house-spirits, mine-spirits or ship-spirits were wholly positive, increasing the self-confidence of men in their work, and encouraging good working practices. And since the sphere of action of these fairies was mundane and practical, encounters with them involved no eeriness, and no hint of erotic seduction.

One strange and haunting variation on the theme of love between a human being and an Otherworld creature is the tradition, known in Ireland, Scotland, the Orkneys and Faroes, and Iceland, that grey seals can take on human form, and mate with men and women. This, it is said, is because they are not really

animals, as is proved by their eyes, which look human; some say they are 'neutral' angels who fell into the sea (see p. 49), or descendants of Pharaoh's soldiers overwhelmed in the Red Sea. Once a year they come ashore to dance in human form, laying their skins aside; if a man steals and hides a seal-girl's skin, she is forced to become his wife. One story is told in all these areas: A man caught a seal-woman in this way, and they lived together for many years, till one day she found her sealskin hidden away and plunged back into the sea to join her true mate, abandoning her human husband and children. In an Icelandic version she laments the choice forced upon her:

Woe is me! Woe is me!
I have seven bairns on land,
And seven in the sea.

In Ireland there are several families alleged to be descended from these matches, notably the Coneelies of Connemara; all are believed to be very skilful fishermen, and it is sometimes added that webbed fingers and/or horny skin is hereditary in their families. Ernest Marwick, discussing Orkney and Shetland lore, wrote:

Unsatisfied mortal women sometimes sought a seal-man lover. If a woman wished to make contact with a selchie, she had to shed seven tears into the sea at high tide. . . . The descendants of a Stronsay woman, who sprang from her union with the seal-man she loved, had a thick horn on the palms of their hands and the soles of their feet. In one of the race, known to the present writer, this was a greenish-white tegument fully a sixteenth of an inch thick which was cracked in places and had a strong fish odour. The old Orkney ballad 'The Great Selchie O' Sule Skerry', of which there are a number of versions, is about the illicit union of a woman and a seal-man.
Ernest Marwick, *The Folklore of Orkney and Shetland,* London, 1974, p. 28.

One of the most archaic figures in European mythology is the Lord, or Lady, of the Beasts. This is a supernatural protector of game animals, who knows each one individually, and without whose permission no hunter can kill any; the Lord, or Lady, must be propitiated and obeyed, and punishes greedy or cruel huntsmen. It is generally agreed that this concept dates from the earliest phase of European society, the pre-agricultural hunting communities, yet there are strong traces of it even in recent folklore. Thus, there is a Swiss cautionary legend collected in 1815, about a chamois hunter climbing a remote peak who was threatened by an angry Dwarf: 'Why have you been killing my chamois so long? You will pay with your blood!' The hunter begged forgiveness, so the Dwarf spared him, and promised to leave one dead chamois every week near the man's hut, provided he killed no other beasts. And so it was, but the hunter, bored at not using his skills, went up the mountain again and was just about to shoot a fine buck when the Dwarf, coming behind him, sent him hurtling down a ravine.

There is a similar tale in Scotland, about the Brown Man of Elsdon Moors, a squat, red-headed dwarf who reproached two boys for shooting game under his protection; one heeded the warning, but the other, who laughed at it, fell ill and died within a year. Also in Scottish lore is a tall, blue-faced crone called the Cailleach Bheur, who is both a personification of winter and a protectress of wild animals, especially deer, wild cattle, and wild goats. A medieval Welsh romance, in *The Mabinogion*, 'The Lady of the Fountain', describes a black, one-eyed giant whose function in the story is simply to test the courage of one of Arthur's knights, but who is called a 'keeper of the forest' and lives surrounded by wild animals:

I asked what power he had over the animals. 'I will show thee, little man,' said he. And he took a club in his hand and with it struck a stag a mighty blow till it gave out a mighty belling. And he looked on them and bade them go graze. And then they bowed down their heads and did him obeisance, even as humble subjects would do to their lord. And he said to me, 'Dost see then, little man, the power I have over these animals?'
The Mabinogion, transl. G. Jones and T. Jones, London, 1949, p. 159.

The Eildon Hills, Roxborough, Scotland. Scene of a famous fifteenth-century romance and a ballad, describing how Thomas the Rhymer (Thomas of Erceldoune) met the Fairy Queen, who took him as her lover and led him to her kingdom inside these hills. He stayed for three years, and returned gifted with powers of poetry and prophecy.

Left. A sixteenth-century wallpainting in the church at Vaxtorp, Sweden, showing the story of the Stolen Drinking Horn. A traveller is accosted by an apparently beautiful and friendly she-troll, who offers him a drink. Instead of swallowing it, he tosses it over his left shoulder and flees, chased by trolls in their true form, till he reaches the safety of a church.

Right. An Irish 'fairy stone' from County Antrim, to be tied to the horns of cows to prevent fairies stealing the milk. Holed stones are a very widespread type of charm, supposedly effective against the evil eye, witchcraft, nightmares, and fairies of all kinds. They may be worn or carried, or hung in buildings. Museum and Art Gallery, Warrington.

Slavonic folklore preserves a detailed version of this archaic motif in the figure of the Vily, the female forest fairies of southern Russia and the Balkans. Vily are primarily tree spirits, but they also rule all wild animals, particularly deer, which they treat like cattle, milking the does and riding on the stags. They attack intruders, especially those who happen to shoot one of their favourite beasts; they can inflict sunstroke, rheumatism, heart attacks, blindness, or insanity. But sometimes they will befriend a man and swear blood-kinship with him, granting him luck in hunting, power over animals, knowledge of healing herbs, and knowledge of hidden treasures. There was a traditional ritual for obtaining these favours. On a Sunday night when the moon is full, the man must go into the forest and sweep a circle round himself with a birch broom, placing in it some horse dung, two or three horse-hairs, and a horse's hoof. After that with his right foot on the hoof, he must hoot three times, then go three times round the hoof, and say: 'O Vily, my blood-sisters, I have sought you through nine fields, nine meadows, nine lakes, nine forests, nine mountains, nine rocky peaks, and nine crumbling castles. Come to me and become my blood-sisters.'

Gifts from Fairies

Folklore reflects hopes as well as fears, one of which is the dream of effortlessly obtaining wealth. Everywhere, it was believed that fairies owned treasures which a man might get hold of if he was very lucky, but that such attempts almost always fail. This theme is well exemplified in Irish traditions about the Leprechán, the fairy cobbler with his pot of gold, as in this nineteenth-century anecdote given by Sir William Wilde:

'Dan of the Leaps' met the Leprechán one morning on Rahona bog. . . . He laid hold of him and swore that he would never part from him till he had given up his treasures. 'Yarrah,' said the little fellow, 'what good is it to you to get them when that fellow behind you will immediately take them from you?' Daniel gave one of his circuitous leaps, but on his turning again to the little fellow he found to his eternal grief that he had scampered off, and was grinning at him from the spray of a bucky briar in the neighbouring hedgerow.
Quoted by Patrick Logan, *The Old Gods: The Facts about Irish Fairies*, Belfast, 1981, p. 69.

A common theme is the transformation of 'fairy gold'. Either seemingly worthless objects such as leaves, ashes or toadstools are given by a fairy to a human, and turn to gold overnight if he is polite enough to keep them; or apparent gold is given to someone undeserving, and quickly turns into leaves or stones. Probably this belief originated in the fact that pots full of cremated bones are found in prehistoric burial mounds; people thought this a fairy trick to disguise gold as rubbish, for who would bother to bury real ashes so carefully?

One such case was reported in the Journal of the Royal Society of Antiquaries in 1854 from near Thomastown in Co. Kilkenny. The mound was opened by a labourer, Thomas Conway, who thought the urn was 'a crock of gold'. In order to force the Good People to take off the spell, he watched the urn until midnight. Then he sacrificed a black cock, which was the recognised method and had been recommended by the best 'fairy doctors' to break the spell. But when he went at cockcrow to see the gold, the burnt bones were still in the pot, so, in his disappointment, he broke the pot in pieces and scattered the contents.
Ibid., p. 73.

There are numerous legends in which men and women who are helpful and polite to fairies are rewarded, while those who are rude, ungrateful or unkind are punished; this is also a constant theme in fictional fairytales. As we have seen already, they can bestow skills as well as gold, and these may become hereditary. One of the commonest is musical skill; in Scandinavian lore, the Näck or Fossegrim who lives in waterfalls is a fine fiddler, and many human players have learnt the art from him, or memorized one of his tunes. The McCrimmons of Skye, the most famous family of pipers in Scotland, are said to have learnt their skill originally from the fairies. Long ago, there was a young McCrimmon whose older brothers would not let him learn the bagpipes (or, in some versions, who was too stupid to learn); a fairy gave him pipes with a silver chanter and taught him a magnificent tune, 'The Finger Lock'.

Another fairy power was that of healing, and knowledge of herbs; practitioners of folk medicine sometimes claimed that they, or an ancestor of theirs, had obtained fairy secrets. In the late seventeenth century, an Irishman named Morough O'Lea was practising physic and surgery in Connaught, though untaught; he owned a fifteenth-century book of medicinal recipes (still extant), which he called 'The Book of Hy Brasil', claiming it had been given him by fairies in Hy Brasil, an Otherworld island. Legend adds that they told him that if he left it unopened for seven years there would be nothing he couldn't cure, but he opened it after only three years, to help victims of an epidemic. Therefore, though a fine healer, he was not able to heal everyone.

As serious belief in fairies diminished among adults, their value as a way of controlling children's behaviour became more prominent. Even in modern England fairy bogies are used as threats, not only to keep children away from dangers but to enforce obedience: 'If you don't go to sleep, Jenny Greenteeth will get you!' – 'You must get home before dark, or the hytersprites will get you!' Rewards, or a combination of expected rewards and punishments, are equally effective. In Bavaria and Austria there is a female figure called Bertha or Perchta, who has been known since the Middle Ages; she roams about at Christmas time, especially on Twelfth Night. In past generations, her chief activities were to punish women and girls who had not finished their annual allotment of spinning, and to see whether children behaved well. Naughty children were told she would carry them into the woods, or slit their stomachs and stuff them with stones and straw, but good children could expect her to leave them small presents, often tossing them in at a window or door. The latter part of the custom continues.

Similarly, there is a pleasant family custom in Britain and America of telling children that if they leave a shed milk-tooth hidden under the pillow or carpet, fairies will take it during the night and leave a coin in exchange. Parents, obviously, ensure that the promise comes true. It is uncertain how old this idea is; it is rarely mentioned in folklore collections, presumably because it seems too commonplace and too light-hearted to interest them. It may have grown out of a traditional belief that house-spirits reward hard-working servant girls by leaving coins in their shoes. In European countries, money is also secretly substituted for a child's tooth, but there it is generally said to be left by a mouse, not a fairy. There is no doubt, however, that the Tooth Fairy flourishes in England; on 12 November 1981, on a television newsreel, the Princess of Wales was glimpsed chatting to a child in a York crowd about the Tooth Fairy, and asking: 'Did a big fairy come along?' and 'Was it 50p or 25p?' Nursery customs will no doubt be the depository for the last shreds of Europe's ancient fairy lore.

Kings and Heroes

From History to Legend

Innumerable battles have been fought between sceptics and believers over the historicity of certain heroic figures. How much truth, if any, lies behind Homer's epics, Arthurian romances, Icelandic sagas, the Robin Hood ballads, the Russian and Yugoslav epic lays? Some dismiss them entirely; others try, often successfully, to sift a few facts from among all the legendary accretions. It is no easy task. Even if the historicity of the central figure is established, the stories about him will range from the demonstrably true, through the plausible but unproven, to the obviously fantastic. Tales that have passed through the processes of oral tradition may retain much reliable information; nevertheless, as Jan Vansina writes concerning present-day fieldwork in Africa:

The initial informant in an oral tradition gives, consciously or unconsciously, a distorted account of what has really happened, because he sees only some aspects of it, and places his own interpretation upon what he has seen. His testimony is stamped by his personality, coloured by his private interests, and set within the frame of reference provided by the cultural values of the society he belongs to. This initial testimony then undergoes alterations and distortions at the hands of all other informants in the chain of transmission, down to and including the very last one. . . .
Jan Vansina, *Oral Tradition*, Harmondsworth, 1973, p. 76.

Historians normally consider only facts, or at least rational deductions from facts, if they can establish them. But folklorists are equally interested in the distortions and fantasies, both from an aesthetic and from a socio-historical point of view. A legend, however untrue, has been shaped by its transmitters into something memorable and emotionally effective; it also reflects communal values, whether for good or ill—pride, nostalgia, the cohesion of a group, propaganda against rival groups, political and moral judgements, and so on. It distorts the original facts, but it reveals how subsequent generations viewed those facts, and why they bothered to remember them.

The folklorist's chief tool in sifting facts from fictions is his awareness of recurrent story-patterns, which makes him sceptical when dealing with incidents which are physically possible but whose frequent repetition undermines their credibility. There are, for instance, too many anecdotes about fugitives who trick pursuers by reversing their horses' shoes, from Dick Turpin to Prince Rákóczi of Hungary, for this motif ever to carry conviction. On the other hand, King Alfred burning the cakes has no exact parallels, only a general resemblance to the humorous misadventures of other kings in disguise; it is therefore more possible (though not very probable) that it could be true. Awareness of patterns is also a protection against tortuous 'explanations' seeking to justify implausible legends. It has, for example, been proposed that the story of Dick Whittington's cat grew out of confusion between French *achat*, 'purchase', and *un chat*, 'a cat'; this misplaced ingenuity collapses when one knows that versions of the cat-selling story occur in Italian, Breton, Norwegian, Danish, Russian and Persian, some dating from the thirteenth century.

Legend-building usually involves fitting pre-existing story-patterns onto the biography of a real person, because they

aptly express some aspect of his personality or achievements. The posthumous glorification of King Olaf Haraldsson of Norway (1016-30) illustrates this well. He had worked vigorously to Christianize his realm, was ousted by rebels, and was killed in battle while trying to regain his power. Almost at once political and religious propaganda began, drawing on commonplaces of hagiography:

Men talked, or it was said that men talked, of the maimed or blind or dead made whole by his blood; and when permission was granted to exhume his body, foreseeably it was found to be uncorrupted. Foreseeably, Bishop Grimkell had him declared a true saint. . . . The miracles increased

The death of a Saxon leader and the destruction of his army by Arthur at the battle of Mount Badon. The battle of Mount Badon (an unidentified site) is the historical core of Arthur's story, from which all his later fame sprang. Archaeology confirms that the Saxon advance into some areas of British territory was checked for a while in the early sixth century. British Library, London.

---

in scope and number, legends grew, stories spread, and it was right and proper for good Norwegians to believe in them. They strengthened the Church and they enhanced the native monarchy.
Gwyn Jones, *A History of the Vikings*, London and New York, 1968, p. 385.

These early stages in building Olaf's legendary reputation were initiated by sections of the upper classes; later, colourful anecdotes from the common international stock of folklore were applied to him. Some told how a giantess, or a troll, hurled rocks at churches he had had built, but missed. One famous tale adapts an old Norse myth about a giant who helped the gods build a fortress, but was cheated of his due pay: A troll once offered to help Olaf build Trondheim Cathedral, if Olaf would give him the sun and the moon when he finished the job. But Olaf found out the troll's secret name, and called out to him by name just as he was completing the spire, thus breaking his power so that he could not finish the

building. Such stories underline Olaf's role as champion of Christianity.

For more ancient heroes, whose real achievements are largely forgotten, legends follow a stereotype so predictable that it has been labelled *the* Hero-Pattern. It is clearest in antiquity (Heracles, Perseus) and for semi-mythical figures (Cuchulainn, Sigurd/Siegfried), but elements from it recur in many contexts. The Hero's conception and birth are peculiar–miraculous, monstrous, or incestuous–and are accompanied by prophecies and portents. His life is threatened in infancy, but he is saved and reared incognito. After initiatory tests, he obtains wonderful weapons. He probably fights monsters and supernatural beings, and/or visits the Otherworld. His love-life (if any) is tragic. His death, preceded by portents,

is dramatic; it may come while fighting against great odds, by treachery, by supernatural intervention, or in fulfilment of a curse. He may disappear, not die; his return may be prophesied.

King Arthur

The British hero best fitting this archetype is Arthur, whose legend has been ramifying for well over a thousand years. The first brief reference to him, in a chronicle compiled around 800 A.D. and attributed to Nennius, lists twelve battles in which he, as leader of Christian Britons, defeated heathen Saxon invaders. The last battle, that at Mount Badon, is now generally accepted as historical, and must have occurred about 500 A.D. Nennius exaggerates Arthur's personal strength, claiming that he killed 960 Saxons single-handed; another section of his chronicle lists various places where marvels may be seen, two of which involve Arthur. The first is a rock at Builth (Wales), bearing the paw-mark of Arthur's hound, imprinted there during a hunt for a boar named Troit. The second, in Herefordshire, is the alleged grave of Arthur's son Amr, whom he himself slew; this may have been a tragic legend like that of Sohrab and Rustum, later unfortunately lost, or it may be the first hint at the story of Mordred, Arthur's nephew/son. The two legends show that the great war-leader of 300 years before had grown into a figure of heroic stature, and a focus for fantasy.

The elaboration of Arthur's story over later centuries is too complex to summarize here; in one source or another, practically all the traits of the Hero-Pattern are ascribed to him. Welsh poems and the *Mabinogion* tell of his hunting a supernatural boar, and fetching a magic cauldron from the Otherworld; they describe his comrades, all great warriors and monster-slayers, and the abduction and rescue of his wife Guenevere. Cornish and Breton traditions were probably equally important, but are lost; their contents can sometimes be deduced from allusions in later writings. In 1136 came Geoffrey of Monmouth's hugely successful (and highly unreliable) *History of the Kings of Britain*. To Arthur's real wars against the Saxons Geoffrey added a fictional war against the Roman empire; more importantly, he introduced social features from his own period (knighthood,

courtly love, tournaments), plus certain themes probably taken from Celtic sources now lost, which thereafter remained essential to Arthur's story. These include: the adulterous and magical circumstances in which he was begotten; his sword, 'forged in the isle of Avalon'; Mordred's treacherous rebellion; and his disappearance after his last battle, when he was 'taken to Avalon for the healing of his wounds, where he gave up the crown of Britain unto his kinsman Constantine.' Next came a flood of French writings; these added the motifs of Arthur's hidden boyhood and the testing by the sword in the stone; the Round Table; and Arthur's unwitting incest with his half-sister which led to Mordred's birth. Wace, a Norman-French poet writing in 1155, comments interestingly on the belief in Arthur's survival, showing that it was no mere literary invention: 'He is still in Avalon, awaited by the Britons, for they say and believe that he will return from the place he went to, and live again.' This, says Wace, is because Merlin foretold that Arthur's end would be 'hidden in doubtfulness'; he adds, 'Men have always doubted, and I am sure will always doubt, whether he is alive or dead.'

The French also began the process of switching attention from Arthur to his knights, some of whom had already figured in Celtic sources, while others

Above. Charlemagne swoons over the body of his nephew Roland, to which an angel has guided him; fourteenth-century illustration to *The Song of Roland*. Biblioteca Nazionale Marciana, Venice.

Right. The Round Table in Castle Hall, Winchester. Radiocarbon analysis dates it to the fourteenth century; probably it was made on the orders of Edward III, who announced in 1344 that he would found an order of knights modelled on Arthur's Company of the Round Table. Its decoration is later; it displays a Tudor Rose, and the portrait of 'Arthur' seems to be a youthful Henry VIII.

(notably Lancelot) were new inventions. Arthur therefore became a more aloof, more passive figure, presiding at banquets and tournaments, and hearing of adventures but rarely undertaking any himself. This reflects a shift in cultural values; the medieval ideal of royalty was more remote and ceremonial than that of the ninth century. The same thing happened in the Charlemagne cycle; the earliest and finest poem, *The Song of Roland*, holds an even balance between the personal prowess of Roland and Oliver and the great battle in which Charlemagne avenges their deaths, whereas in later poems about Ogier the Dane or Huon of Bordeaux, the Emperor stays in the background. At the same time, the emphasis on Arthur's knights led to a new tragic theme: the disintegration of the fellowship of the Round Table,

which dominates Malory's treatment. This, however, belongs to literary history, not folk traditions.

Malory knew of the rumours that Arthur would return:

. . . yet some men say in many parts of England that King Arthur is not dead, but had by the will of our Lord Jesus Christ into another place; and men say that he shall come again, and he shall win the Holy Cross. I will not say that it shall be so, but rather I will say, here in this world he changed his life. But many men say there is written upon his tomb this verse: Hic jacet Arthurus, Rex quondam Rexque futurus.
Thomas Malory, *Le Morte d'Arthur*, Everyman Edition, London, 1906, vol. II, p. 391.

Many took the myth of Arthur's return seriously, and it had political overtones. In 1113 there was a riot in Cornwall when French monks laughed at it. In 1191, a grave alleged to be Arthur's was displayed at Glastonbury, probably as part of a campaign to crush Welsh nationalism by proving him to be dead. The Tudors, however, encouraged interest in Arthur to support their claim, as Welshmen, to rule Britain; Henry VII named his eldest son Arthur and stressed that he had been born at Winchester, home of the Round Table. In later folklore one finds a recurrent

local legend claiming that Arthur is sleeping in some cave (usually an imaginary one) from which he will emerge in some hour of national peril; it is generally said that someone once briefly entered the cave, and saw the king and his knights asleep, surrounded by weapons and treasures. Variants of the tale are told at Sewingshields (Northumberland), Alderley Edge (Cheshire), Richmond (Yorkshire), and Craig y Ddinas (Gwynedd).

Sleeping Heroes

There are very many rulers of whom it is said that they are asleep and will return as saviours—among others, Charle-

magne, King Sebastian of Poland, the Emperors Barbarossa and Frederick II in Germany, Holger Danske in Denmark, the O'Neills in Ireland, Queen Jadwiga in Poland, Prince Marko in Serbia, King Matyas in Hungary. There is a natural reluctance to admit that some beloved leader really has died, but this persistent theme also owes much to Christian prophecies which circulated in medieval Europe, claiming that a 'Last Emperor' would emerge from hiding shortly before the End of the World, to fight Antichrist and prepare for the Millenium. This mysterious figure was identified with various dead rulers, whose return was awaited. Charlemagne, for instance, was thought to have been a persistent enemy of Islam, whereas in reality most of his wars were against Saxons; by the end of the eleventh century it was even thought that he had ruled in Jerusalem, and popular preachers foretold that he would return to lead a Crusade. He was said to be sleeping in his vault at Aachen, or else inside some mountain. Even in the late Middle Ages and Renaissance, prophecies circulated about a 'Second Charlemagne' who would conquer all the world and visit the Holy Sepulchre.

In Germany, many refused to accept the deaths of Frederick Barbarossa (1190) and his grandson Frederick II (1250). The latter in particular was said to be living in exile, or as a pilgrim or hermit, who would return to inaugurate the Millenium. There were rebellions of the poor in the 1280s, led by pseudo-

Fredericks; they were defeated and executed, but in the fourteenth century people still expected Frederick's return, saying that Prester John had given him a potion to keep him young, and a ring to make him invisible. In 1434, there was still a 'heresy' claiming that he would live until the end of the world 'and that there has been and shall be no proper Emperor but he.' German folk tradition asserts that he is hidden inside Mount Kyffhausen:

When he emerges, he will hang his shield on a leafless tree, the tree will sprout green leaves, and a better age will begin. Usually, he sits at a bench at a round stone table, resting his head on his hand, sleeping, nodding his head and blinking his eyes. His beard has grown long–according to some, right through the stone table. But according to others, the beard grows round the table, and when it has encircled it three times it will be the time of his awakening. It has now grown around twice.
Donald Ward, vol. I, p. 33.

Such legends are a powerful focus for the hopes of an oppressed nation or class. The Hungarian Prince Rácóczi died in exile in 1735, after the failure of his eight-year struggle to free Hungary from Austrian rule, yet long afterwards it was being said that he had not really died–he was waiting till foals are born with teeth and crucifixes move, when he would come to lead his people in an hour of need.

Ideal Warriors

Most legendary heroes are warriors, whether their warfare belongs to known history or is semi-mythicized. Among the latter is the Irish Cuchulainn, who may or may not have lived in first-century Ulster; every story about him exalts his superhuman skill and ferocity, sometimes in such fantastic terms that scholars have suggested that he was originally divine. In battle, his whole face and body grew distorted, blood spurted from his head, his forehead emitted a fiery ray, and he grew so hot that he had to be cooled in three vats of cold water before he ceased to be a danger even to his own comrades.

Equally remarkable is a Nordic hero, Bothvar Bjarki, supposedly one of the retinue of a historical Danish king. The core of his legend was a heroic lay (now lost) in which he exhorted his comrades to battle, though desperately outnumbered; he also had the superhuman power of turning himself into a bear at will, and when in this guise would trample men and horses underfoot and crunch them between his teeth. Heroes such as this cannot be defeated by mere human foes; Bothvar and his companions were doomed by Odin, god of war, and later versions add that their enemies used sorcery to send reanimated corpses into battle against them.

Cuchulainn too was destroyed by supernatural forces, being tricked into breaking magical taboos on which his luck depended, and being hounded by the war-goddess Morrigan. For him, as for most heroes, death is the climax of his grandeur; an eighth-century text tells how he met his end, having been mortally wounded by a spear-thrust in the belly:

Cuchulainn gathered up his entrails in his arms. . . . He went towards a standing stone on the plain. He put his belt round it so that he would not die sitting or lying down—so that he would die standing. The men surrounded him. They did not dare go towards him. They thought he was alive. . . .

Then a raven flew onto Cuchulainn's shoulder. 'That pillar did not use to bear birds,' said Erc mac Coipri. So then Lugaid gathered up Cuchalainn's hair from behind and struck off his head. Cuchulainn's sword fell from his hand and struck Lugaid's right hand to the ground. Maria Tymoczko, *Two Death Tales from the Ulster Cycle*, Dublin, 1981, pp. 60-1.

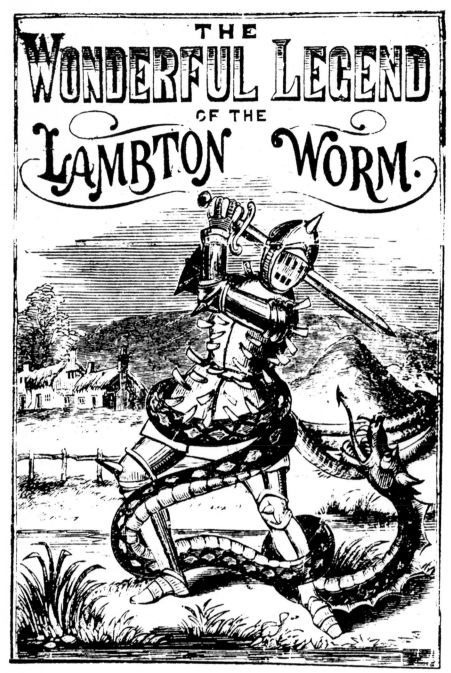

THE WONDERFUL LEGEND OF THE LAMBTON WORM.

Oddly, one man who in real life was a superb war-leader, Alexander the Great, is celebrated in medieval and modern legend for quite other exploits. The process began with *The Romance of Alexander, c.* 300 A.D., which invented many colourful adventures for him: for instance, that he explored the sea-bed in a glass diving-bell, and trained gryphons to draw his chariot up into the sky. Some medieval writers expanded these science-fiction exploits, while others sent Alexander on exotic journeys to lands of giants, and of dog-headed or bird-headed men, where he gathered extraordinary jewels and herbs. In modern Balkan folklore the favourite theme is Alexander and the Water of Immortality; there are many versions, in all of which he finds the water but is thwarted at the last minute when someone else unwittingly drinks it. Usually it is his sister, who is therefore transformed into an immortal and dangerous mermaid.

Hero legends, like myths, are full of monster-slayings, particularly the killing of dragons. The best-known early European dragon-slayers (saints excluded) are Germanic: Beowulf and Sigurd (Siegfried) the Volsung. This exploit of Sigurd's is the one stable element in the complicated and contradictory tales told of him in Scandinavia and in Germany. The Nordic version, constantly alluded to in early poetry and sculpture, tells how he was induced to kill the dragon Fafnir, by an evil dwarf who meant to double-cross and kill him after eating the dragon's heart, which could magically confer wisdom. The dwarf told Sigurd to cook the heart, but while doing so he burned his finger, licked it, and found himself suddenly able to understand the language of birds; a bird advised him to kill the treacherous dwarf and take the dragon's gold. German sources omit

this; instead, they say Sigurd became invulnerable by bathing in the dragon's blood.

Dragon-slaying has remained to this day a popular theme for local legends throughout Europe; Britain alone has over seventy variants. The heroes are not great national figures; they may be ancestors of local aristocratic landowning families, or vague anonymous medieval knights, or locally venerated saints. Frequently, at least in Britain, the dragon-slayer is said to be a local working man – shepherd, blacksmith, farmworker – or an outlaw or criminal. The slaying is sometimes by combat,

echoing ancient heroic models, but more often it is achieved by some picturesque and ingenious trick, usually rather comic in effect. The hero may dress in spiked armour which rips the dragon to pieces when he coils round the hero, or swallows him; he may choke the dragon with peat-smoke, poison him, give him indigestible food, or kill him in his sleep. These humorous and 'unsporting' devices are not, as might be supposed, a modern development; trickery has always been an acceptable theme in mythology and heroic tales – Greek myths include many examples, notably the ruses used by

Perseus to defeat the Gorgon.

Legend-building does not consist only in the introduction of supernatural or fantastic elements into tales about historical figures; indeed, these may be wholly absent. More essential is the way historical facts are compressed, dramatized, and interpreted for maximum emotional effect. This is exemplified by the Yugoslav poems about the battle of Kosovo (1389) in which Prince Lazar was defeated and killed by Turks. The disaster is blamed upon a personal feud between two nobles, Miloš and Vuk, which is regarded as a matter of family honour: the wives of the two men, both daughters of Prince Lazar, quarrel; Miloš consequently strikes Vuk; in revenge, Vuk convinces Lazar that Miloš is disloyal, with the result that when Miloš is surrounded by enemies on the battlefield, Lazar refuses to rescue him; thus Miloš is slain, after prodigies of valour, the battle is lost, and Lazar too is slain. Some poems allege (quite wrongly) that Vuk was a traitor in league with the Turks. The Kosovo lays, like *The Song of Roland*, transmute a national defeat into a story of tragic but honorable misjudgements by heroes, and black treachery by a single villain.

Certain warriors are famous also for their love affairs, which generally end tragically. This theme owes something to a pre-Christian belief that war-goddesses take heroes as their lovers. In Norse tradition Sigurd's love for Bryn-hild probably originated in a re-lationship of this type, though surviving versions often confuse matters by alternating between presenting Bryn-hild as a supernatural Valkyrie and seeing her as a betrayed and vengeful human princess. The chief concern of the heroic love-legends, however, is with conflicts of loyalty and honour, as in the Irish tales about Diarmuid's elopement with Grainne, wife of his uncle and overlord Finn, and Noise's elopement with Deirdre, wife of his uncle and overlord King Conchobar. In each instance, the young man is forced, by honour or through magic, to accept the woman's proffered love and thus break allegiance; the lovers flee, but later the hero is killed by the wronged husband; the woman is left to mourn. In these early prototypes, the story is an essentially masculine tragedy about broken faith, broken friendship, and the needless death of a fine warrior. Later, in medieval romances about Lancelot and Guenevere, Tristan and Isolda, emphasis shifts to the lovers themselves–the tricks they use in order to meet, the delicate emotions they feel. In the Tristan story, particularly, the husband, King Mark, is stupid and unpleasant, so that all sympathy is concentrated on the lovers; moreover, once this legend was incorporated into the Arthurian cycle, Tristan's feudal allegiance is to Arthur, not Mark, which eliminates one aspect of his dilemma.

Fugitives and Outlaws

Being at odds with their overlords, Diarmuid and Tristan live as fugitives, repeatedly evading capture by ingenuity or luck, which adds greatly to the appeal of their stories. Exciting escapes are a constant motif in legends, whether historically based or not; fugitives escaping through secret tunnels, or by the assistance of devoted women, wandering in disguise, hiding in caves, leaping to freedom from tower win-dows or off cliff-tops, can be found in all national traditions. William Tell's story ends with a mighty leap to freedom, from a ship onto a lakeside rock still called Tell's Slab. Robert the Bruce, during his early years of wander-ing, is said (like so many others) to have baffled pursuers by shoeing his horse backwards, and to have been saved while hiding in a cave by the fact that a spider spun a web across the entrance, so that the place seemed undisturbed. Owen Glendower is credited with climbing a sheer gully in Snowdonia to escape capture. The historically ac-curate account of Charles II hiding in an oak after the battle at Boscobel led storytellers in Sussex to invent num-erous imitative concealments in trees along his route to the coast.

Many legends concern outlaws and bandits–an ambiguous category includ-ing both heroes and villains, and ranging from idealized rebels and freedom-fighters, through picturesquely chivalrous robbers, to clever tricksters, or to bloodthirsty murderers or even cannibals (e.g. the Scottish Sawney Bean). Elements of political and social protest are often present when legend presents bandits and outlaws in a favourable light. Robin Hood has now become universally known as one who 'robbed the rich to give to the poor', though curiously enough this feature is not much emphasized in the original

ballads; there, Robin and his men usually keep for themselves the booty they wrest from the rich, and only in one or two instances does a poor man benefit from their activities. The main appeal of the ballads is in the vigorous fights, the archery, the idyllic picture of the 'merry greenwood', and the amusing contrast between Robin's criminal behaviour and his polished manners. The 'gentlemanly' robber is a common figure in legend; Dick Turpin and other highwaymen are often cast in this role.

The political relevance of outlaw legends is greatest where there have been guerrilla wars against foreign oppressors, as in the Balkans under Austrian and Turkish rule, for there bandits are easily identified with patriotic freedom fighters. In Greece such men are known as *klefts* (literally, 'robbers'); in Bulgaria and Yugoslavia as *hajduks*, in Hungary as *betyars*; ballads and anecdotes celebrate their courage, strength, sense of honour, and love of freedom. In the Hungarian War of Independence (1848) the *betyars*, outlaw bands of the forests and plains, offered their help to Lajos Kossuth and fought as guerrillas. After Kossuth's cause was lost, they reverted to banditry, but their patriotic role is recalled in traditional tales which still circulate. There is an anecdote recorded in 1947 about an encounter between Kossuth and the famous outlaw Sándor Rózsa which is rather like some of the Robin Hood ballads; ruler and outlaw recognize each other's worth, while the local representative of 'law and order' is a ridiculous coward. But the authentic historical context of the Hungarian tale raises it to a much higher level of interest than the English one:

When people all over the world had been stirred to rebellion, Lajos Kossuth betook himself to Sándor Rózsa and his gang of outlaws. He said to them, 'Look here! I want your help.'

It was in the company of the Chief Justice of Szeged that Kossuth went to the haunts of Sándor Rózsa. All along the way, the Chief Justice was trembling in every limb, in such deadly fear was he of Sándor Rózsa and his gang.

On their arrival, the outlaws closed up around them and began shouting, 'Out with your money! We want your money!'

But when Sándor Rózsa drew closer and recognised Lajos Kossuth, he stepped up to his men and slapped their faces. Then he led the king into his hideout. Heaps of treasure were there, as may be imagined, and from it he gave an amount to the king.
Linda Dégh, *Folktales of Hungary*, London and Chicago, 1965, pp. 223-4.

In Greece, the deeds of the bandit-guerrillas, the *klefts*, inspired many folksongs from the seventeenth, eighteenth and nineteenth centuries. A few may have been composed by the bandits themselves boasting of their deeds, but the events described were often of such strictly localized importance that it is difficult to find evidence by which to assess their reliability as history. Obvious fictional motifs are often present: amazing feats of strength; girls disguising themselves as bandits and showing exemplary valour; lamentations over dying heroes. The poems stress and dramatize these deaths; if a *kleft* falls in battle, it will be against overwhelming odds, but far more frequently he is treacherously slain during a truce, or murdered by a trusted friend.

Anti-heroes

So far, we have considered men who are heroes in both senses of the term: they are central figures in stories, and they are held up for admiration. But folklore has 'anti-heroes' too—figures who are morally condemned, yet whose legends are widely known. Indeed their immorality and their tragic fates make a particularly strong appeal to writers, artists and musicians, so that several have passed from folk tradition into upper-class culture. Faust, who will be discussed in the next chapter, is in this category. So is Don Juan, a real person with a reputation as a seducer, whose sudden death was popularly linked to a pre-existing folktale about a man who recklessly invites a corpse, skeleton, or graveyard statue to dinner, with disastrous results to himself. The stories of Faust and Juan were exploited in popular media such as puppet plays and chapbooks, as dreadful warnings of the fates of sinners.

The most elaborate and most widely known popular legend of an accursed 'hero', a living example of Divine punishment, is the story of the Wandering Jew—or, in German, the 'Eternal Jew'. It is first mentioned by a medieval English monk, Matthew Paris, of St Alban's Abbey. In 1228 an Armenian Archbishop was visiting the Abbey, and the monks questioned him about rumours that there was a man alive in the world, called Joseph, who had been present when Christ suffered. The Archbishop said this was quite true, and he had seen the man himself; he had been a porter in Pilate's court, and his

original name had been Cartaphilus. Seeing Christ being dragged from the court, he had struck him and jeered: 'Go quicker, Jesus, why are you loitering?' Jesus replied sternly, 'Yes, I am going; you will wait till I return.' Consequently Cartaphilus, though repentant and baptized (as Joseph), cannot die; when he reaches a hundred he is restored to the exact age he was when Christ spoke, namely thirty.

This story persisted through the Middle Ages, but became far more influential after the publication in Germany in 1602 of a chapbook entitled *A Short Description of a Jew Named Ahasuerus*, reprinted in many countries in various versions. It identifies Ahasuerus as a cobbler who refused to let Christ rest his cross against the wall of his shop on the road to Calvary, and so must never rest till Doomsday; his fate, which he humbly accepts, makes him a living warning to unbelievers, especially to Jews. The story seems to have been commonly accepted as true. Chapbooks and other sources repeatedly allege that the wanderer has been recently seen—at Lubeck in 1601, Paris in 1604, Hamburg in 1614 or 1616 and again in 1633, Brussels in 1640, Stamford in 1658, and so on. Imposters may have adopted the role to obtain money from the credulous.

The tradition lingered long. In a Welsh village in the nineteenth century, as the folklorist Mary Trevelyan recorded, a handsome stranger who jilted a local girl was suspected of being the Wandering Jew, since on leaving her he had said, 'It is my fate to win love; it is my doom never to marry.' In some regions, the Jew takes on superhuman attributes. In Spain, he is a giant; in Switzerland, his tears are said to have formed a lake near Zermatt; in Brittany, a sudden strong wind means that he is passing invisibly; in Italy, some say he is chained to the bottom of the sea, others that he is eternally digging a pit to Hell. In bleak mountainous regions in Germany, Switzerland and France, it is commonly said that perpetual ice and snow mark the places where he treads. Often, it is said, he reveals his identity by alluding to long forgotten events; or, on visiting a small village, he remarks that when he last passed that way, a hundred years before, it was a rich and prosperous town, and prophesies that in another hundred years it will have vanished utterly.

It is quite common to find folk legends drawing upon real or invented details of Christ's life—and especially of his childhood or his passion—to explain alleged punishments or curses on individuals or groups; several stories of

Right. Tristan brings home Isolde (Iseult) to be the bride of his uncle King Mark. Behind them stands Isolde's maid, who had brewed a love potion for the wedding night; Tristan and Isolde unwittingly drank it themselves, and fell irrevocably in love. Musée Condé, Chantilly.

Left. The Flying Dutchman. An illustration to Wagner's opera, which popularized the legend.

this type were given in Chapter Two, and another, concerning La Befana, will be mentioned in Chapter Eight (p. 128). The figure of the Wandering Jew, however, achieved a fame and a mythical stature far beyond the rest, for it symbolically expressed what medieval Christians believed, in all seriousness, was God's intention for the Jewish race. It was thought that the Jews as a whole were doomed to be homeless wanderers for ever as punishment for their part in Christ's death, but that eventually, shortly before the End of the World, they would repent and be baptized. The legend of the Wandering Jew encapsulates this belief; it also warns everyone, Christians included, about the wickedness of blasphemy and cruelty—many chapbook versions include episodes where the Wanderer rebukes Christian sinners.

In later centuries the story took on other meanings. To nineteenth century romantics the Wandering Jew ceased to be a specifically religious figure and became a nobly suffering outcast, victim of inexplicable fate. Parallel stories grew up. At the popular level, there was the Flying Dutchman, doomed to sail for ever in punishment for blasphemously swearing he would sail round Cape Horn 'whether it was God's will or not'. In literature, the doom and repentence and urge to repeated confession which Coleridge ascribes to his Ancient Mariner echo the older legend. But to the Nazis, the story of the Wandering Jew was ideal propaganda; in June 1933 one of their newspapers declared:

We must build up our State without Jews. They can never be anything but stateless aliens, they can never have any legal or constitutional status. Only by this means can Ahasuerus be forced once again to take up his wanderer's staff.
Völkischer Beobachter, 26 June 1933, quoted by Venetia Newall, 'The Jew as Witch Figure', in *The Witch Figure*, ed. V. Newall, London, 1973, p. 101.

Rarely can folk tradition have been put to more sinister use.

Wonder-workers: Saints, Seers, Magicians

The Powers of Holy Men

Most societies hold that some people, though wholly human, have power to perform miraculous deeds and to communicate with, or even control, spirits, otherworld beings, and the dead. These powers may be regarded as gifts from God, or from some other non-human being, either good or evil; or as inborn qualities; or as achieved by occult studies or ascetic practices. The source matters far less than whether the powers are used for the benefit of the community or for its harm; this chapter will deal mostly with benevolent wonder-workers, and the next with those who are harmful.

In Christian Europe, the commonest beneficent wonder-workers are of course the saints; it is particularly interesting to note the similarities between the achievements ascribed to them in life and after death, and archaic stories and beliefs from non-Christian contexts. For instance, there is an archetypal life-story for a legendary saint, as there is for a hero, and the two have much in common. The saint's birth is preceded and accompanied by prophecies and marvels; he shows precocious wisdom and piety, parallelling the strength of some heroes in infancy; he owns miracle-working objects (crozier, bell, stole, etc.) corresponding to the hero's marvellous weapons; he battles against demons and/or human persecutors. Some saints become rulers, as kings, bishops or abbots. Others die as martyrs, their courage under torture being as elaborately stressed as the deaths of epic heroes, for in both cases a fine death crowns life's glory. After death, however, the typical saintly legend diverges from the Hero-Pattern, since a saint's body, unlike a hero's, has miraculous

and protective power; his tomb becomes a cult centre, his relics are distributed, his feast-day is instituted. In pagan Greece and Rome there had been similar honours for heroes, but Christian Europe reserved them for saints—and for a few national heroes, such as Charlemagne and El Cid, who were locally regarded as uncanonized saints, and to whom posthumous miracles were occasionally attributed.

The Church tried to ensure that persons honoured as saints were not mere fictions, and were worthy of the title. By the twelfth century, canonization could only be authorized at Rome, after long investigations; even in earlier times, when saints were created in their own regions by popular acclaim, a bishop's endorsement was needed (as for Olaf of Norway, mentioned in the previous chapter). The *Life of St Martin*, the Bishop of Tours, written *c.* 400, describes how he doubted the authenticity of a martyr at whose grave an earlier bishop had allowed an altar to be set up. He inquired into the martyr's name and dates, and on getting only vague, incoherent replies, grew 'worried and uneasy'; eventually he prayed publicly at the tomb, asking God to reveal who lay there. At once he saw 'a loathsome, fierce shadow' (invisible to everyone else), which confessed that in life it had been a brigand, not a martyr, executed for its crimes, and deserving no veneration. St Martin had the tomb removed, 'and thus delivered the people from the error of their superstition'.

The development of legends, unfortunately, was less rigorously controlled. Accounts of the agonies of martyrs, the austerities of hermits, the posthumous apparitions and miracles of all categories of saint, grew ever more elaborate, largely because the prestige

of churches, monasteries and pilgrimage centres depended on that of their patron saints, and competition was fierce. Motifs were copied from one biography or miracle-book into another, creating stereotypes as predictable as those of fairytales; staffs that blossom; wild animals that feed or protect a hermit; statues that fall from the sky, or float ashore in empty boats; saints who cross the sea on their outstretched cloak; waggons which halt miraculously to show where a saint must be buried, or a church built. Some vivid episodes are drawn from folktale motifs, as when St Elizabeth of Hungary receives a ring from her husband which will break if he dies while on a Crusade. The belief in fairy changelings is unexpectedly adapted for use in no fewer than three saints' lives (Lawrence, Bartholomew, and Stephen the First Martyr), in texts from the tenth to the fourteenth century. Each of them, it is said, was stolen in infancy by a demon and abandoned in some wild place, where a pious man found and reared him; the demon, meanwhile, either took the baby's place himself or laid a magic puppet in the cradle. This imp, like all changelings, 'refused to grow, and cried in his cradle day and night'; one version claims that fourteen wet-nurses died of exhaustion from trying to feed it. Eventually the saint, now grown up, returns home, reveals who he is, and unmasks the imp, which flees. Interestingly, one illustration to the legend of St Stephen shows the puppet-imp being burnt, as changelings sometimes were.

Sometimes ancient tales were adopted almost unaltered, notably that of Oedipus unwittingly killing his father and marrying his mother. This is told of Judas Iscariot, appalling crimes being evidently thought appropriate to him.

More surprisingly, it is also told of several saints, to show how God brings good out of evil. The version concerning Gregory the Great is the best known, having been taken up into literature by the medieval German poet Hartmann von Aue. According to this, Gregory was the son of incestuous twins, who soon repented and set their baby adrift in an open boat. He became a knight, and though he did not kill his father as Oedipus did, he did meet and marry his widowed mother. When the truth came out he had himself marooned on a bare rock, where he lived for seventeen years in such hardships that he shrivelled into a little creature like a hedgehog. Eventually, his sanctity having been revealed in

visions, he was elected Pope, and used his authority to absolve his mother of her double incest; she and the daughters she had borne him became nuns.

The marvellous powers ascribed to many saints are often parallelled in the holy men of other cultures, particularly in Muslim and Buddhist mysticism and in archaic shamanistic traditions. Thus, holiness is widely associated with an ability to master extreme heat and cold, and to emit spiritual energy in the form of light. Cicero alludes to tales about ascetic sages in the Caucasus who lived naked in the snow, and could fling themselves into fire 'without a moan'; in modern times, the same is often said about Tibetan monks. Among the many Christian examples are St Cainnicus

and Blessed Marianus Scotus, who needed no candle when writing at night, for their fingers became luminous; the hermit Abbot Lot, whose fingers resembled ten fiery torches when he prayed; St Wenceslas, whose footprints melted snow; St Catherine of Sienna, whose hand was so hot it made water boil. Indeed, the artistic convention of giving saints haloes originated from belief in their power to emit radience. Other saintly powers with many non-Christian parallels are bilocation (the ability to project one's 'astral body' through space, and so be seen in two places at once); walking on water; and levitation, the ability to rise into the air during ecstatic prayer. The most famous saintly levitator was St Joseph of Cupertino (1603-63), a Franciscan friar. Eyewitnesses claimed to have seen him float into the air in the middle of the church and fly to clasp the tabernacle of the high altar; on another occasion he flew up into an olive tree and remained kneeling for half an hour on a gently swaying branch. As he flew, he gen-

erally shrieked loudly; the other friars found this so disturbing that for thirty years Joseph was banned from the refectory, the choir, and all processions.

Saints were often thought able miraculously to control wild beasts; on the religious level this symbolized the ability to curb physical passions through asceticism, but it inevitably gave rise to picturesque stories. Thus, St Sergius of Radonezh, a Russian hermit who lived in a forest, shared his bread with a bear-cub; St John Koutouzelis, a thirteenth century monk on Mount Athos, sang so sweetly that goats danced around him; St Mamas of Cyprus is shown on icons riding a lion and leading a lamb, like the 'little child' in Isaiah. St Patrick banishing the snakes, and St Francis taming the wolf and preaching to birds, are examples well known to this day. Sometimes, extremely repulsive animals (snakes, scorpions, dragons) symbolize the devil, and are destroyed by the saint. The commonest is the dragon; there are said to be over forty saints in the Latin

Church alone, excluding Orthodox and Armenian ones, whose legendary exploits include dragon-slaying. Even female saints kill or tame dragons, by making the sign of the cross or binding them with their girdle, which symbolizes chastity; some male saints kill them in combat, as St George allegedly did, while others use prayer, holy water, or simply a word of command. The identification of devil and dragon, based on *Revelations XX.*2, permeates hagiography and religious art; it has been enriched by motifs from folklore, e.g. the rescue of a princess from being devoured, and in return has contributed to the remarkable persistence of dragon-slaying in popular story-telling.

The commonest power was that of healing, which, unlike the others, grew even stronger after death. It was popularly supposed that every saint in Heaven specialized in curing one particular disease, though there was naturally some local variation and overlapping. Protestants such as Reginald Scot mocked the system:

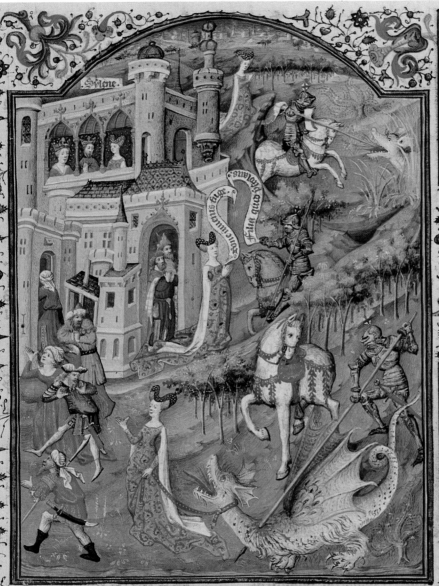

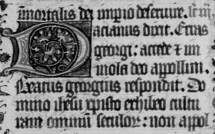

puincia huc aduenisti: vel quo
nomine uoeris. Sanctus ge
orgius dixit. Xpianus + dei
seruus sum: georgius nuncu
por genere capadocus puie mee
comitatum gerens. Elegi uero
temporali carere dignitate: et

imortalis dei unpio deseruire. se in
acianus dixit. Eruas
georgi: accede + im
mola deo apollini.
Seatus georgius respondit. Do
mino ihesu xpisto exhibeo culti
ram omnui seculox: non appol

*S. John and S. Valentine excelled at
the falling evil, S. Roch was good at
the plague, S. Petronill at the ague.
As for S. Margaret, she passed Lucina
for a midwife . . . in which respect S.
Marpurge is joined with her in
commission. For madmen and such as
are possessed with devils, S. Romane
was excellent, and Friar Ruffine was
also pretty skilful in that art. For
botches and biles, Cosmas and
Damian; S. Clare for the eyes; S.
Appoline for teeth; S. Job for the
pox. And for sore breasts, S. Agatha.*
Reginald Scot, *Discoverie of
Witchcraft: A Discourse of Divels*,
1584, ch. 24.

These specializations sometimes corresponded to real or legendary events in
the saint's life; St Appoline had had her
teeth pulled out as a torture, while St
Margaret, having been swallowed by a
dragon, split it open from inside and
stepped out unharmed—a safe delivery!
Others involve puns; St Clare's name is
in several languages a homonym for
'clear', so she bestows clear sight, and
also clear weather. Others are pure
misunderstandings; St Anthony's fame
for finding lost objects apparently arose
from a hymn which said he 'found the
lost', i.e. reclaimed sinners. By the end
of the Middle Ages every aspect of daily
life was under the aegis of some saint;
each trade had its patron, every danger
its averter; there were saints to cure
farm animals, expel vermin, protect
crops, quench fires, divert storms, and
so on. Their benevolence, exerted from
Heaven, was focussed on earth through
their relics and shrines, and through the
medals, statues and symbolic objects
associated with their cult which people
wore or displayed as protective talismans. To Protestants, such practices
were deplorable superstitions; to Catholics they were—and in many countries
still are—a normal expression of religious faith.

Village Seers and Healers

What neither Catholic nor Protestant
theology could tolerate, however, was
that people should turn in their troubles
to seers and healers in their own
communities, even though these 'con-

jurers' and 'wise women' used their
alleged powers beneficially, and generally regarded themselves as specially
gifted by God. To churchmen of all
denominations, such powers were suspect, and might just as easily come from
devils as from God. Moreover, the

Church had decided early in the Middle
Ages that there were no 'neutral' spirits,
so that everything not obviously an
angel must be a demon; consequently,
anyone who observed such folk traditions as hanging rags on fairy trees or
putting food out for house-spirits could

be accused of 'worshipping' demons.

Medieval documents afford some glimpses of the ensuing misunderstandings. Around 1235 a Dominican Inquisitor at Lyons, Stephen de Bourbon, discovered that mothers with sickly babies were consulting an old woman who was taking them to a holy well in a forest, dedicated to St Guinefort. There they 'made offerings of salt and other things', hung the baby's swaddling clothes on bushes, and passed the naked baby to one another nine times, between two tree-trunks. The old woman and the mother would then leave the baby alone for a while under a tree, 'calling upon the fauns in the forest to take the sick, feeble child, which, they said, was theirs, and to return their own child which the fauns had taken away.' To us, it is clear that the local 'wise woman' was practising a ritual to induce fairies to re-exchange a changeling; some of its elements are familiar down to the nineteenth century, e.g. passing sick children through split tree-trunks or holed stones. But Stephen, following the usual assumptions of medieval theologians, identified the fairies with pagan Roman fauns, and hence with devils; to him, the women were guilty of 'making offerings to demons'. Further enquiries uncovered further scandal. In the minds of the local population, 'St Guinefort' was not the martyr of that name honoured at Pavia and elsewhere, but a dog—a brave greyhound, unjustly killed on suspicion of having attacked his master's child, whom in fact he had saved from a snake. The holy well and the trees marked the dog's grave. This legend is an international one, best known in a Welsh version, 'The Hound Gelert'; how it came to be confused with a saint's cult is as puzzling to the folklorist as to the shocked Stephen, who reacted energetically:

We had the dead dog disinterred, and the sacred wood cut down and burnt, along with the remains of the dog. And I had an edict passed by the lords of the estate, warning that anyone going henceforth to that place for any such reason would be liable to have his possessions seized and sold.

Jean-Claude Schmitt, *The Holy Greyhound: Guinefort, Healer of Children*, Cambridge, 1983, p. 6.

But there is also occasional evidence of amiable co-operation between medieval clergy and local seers. At Montaillou, a French Pyrenean village investigated in 1318-25 by Inquisitors seeking Cathar heretics, lived a certain Arnaud Gélis, part-time sacristan and servant to the village priest, who was also what was there called 'a messenger of souls'. He had the gift of being able to see the dead who, according to local belief, ran over hill and dale, rushing from church to

Above. An image of Our Lady of the Seven Dolours (symbolized by seven swords in her heart), surrounded by *ex votos* – i.e. wax or silver models of limbs, hearts, or heads bought and donated to the shrine in thanksgiving for cures.

Right. The well of Notre Dame de Rancier, Josselin, Brittany. Holy wells are important centres of pilgrimage for Bretons, most are dedicated to Our Lady or to her mother St Anne, who is equally venerated.

church in penance for their sins, in great torment, and longing to attain 'the place of rest', i.e. Heaven. It was the task of Gélis, and others like him, to take messages from the dead to the living, and vice versa. The dead would remind the living of their duty to have Masses said for their repose, to give alms to the poor, and to ensure that oil-lamps burned in the churches all night to comfort visiting souls. (No doubt Gélis, as sacristan, saw to it that this was done, once the relatives had paid for the oil.) Furthermore, since the dead were believed to know everything, people would seek information from them, through Gélis, on such matters as the whereabouts of an absent son who had not been heard from for some time. In payment for his services, Gélis received food, drink, or a little money. His master the priest approved of his activities; the Inquisitors did not.

Parson 'Conjurers'

Priests themselves were often regarded in folk tradition as wonder-workers, partly because one of their tasks was to expel demons by blessings and exorcisms (a process easily confused with a magician's ability to order demons to serve him), and partly because their literacy and knowledge of Latin and Greek overawed the peasantry. In Catholic times a famous priest might be regarded almost as a saint, as was John Schorne, Rector of North Marston, (Buckinghamshire) from 1290 to 1314; he was a great exorcist, and is said to have forced a devil to enter one of his boots and held him captive there. After his death pilgrims flocked to his grave, and to a well he was said to have created by striking the earth with his staff; in 1475 his body was removed from Marston to St George's Chapel, Windsor, where his cult became even more popular. Had it not been for the Reformation, he would probably have eventually been canonized.

Post-Reformation English folklore contains plenty of colourful tales about parsons who exorcize evil spirits, generally dangerous ghosts, but they are regarded as godly and helpful magicians, not as saints. Such anecdotes, which are numerous in the western counties of England, imply a wish that the clergy would use spiritual power to put a stop to hauntings; in real life, however, exorcisms were hardly ever performed by the Anglican clergy, so people troubled by the supernatural could only turn to the village 'cunning man'. In contrast, the ghost-laying parson of legend proceeds with admirable vigour. He confronts the spectre,

which is aggressive and frequently in the form of a huge animal, and recites psalms and prayers at it, while holding a candle. Sometimes several parsons join forces, and a congregation assembles; the prayers may be in Latin or Hebrew; magic circles may be used. Gradually the ghost shrinks, till it is small and weak and can be driven into a bottle, snuff-box, or boot, which the parson throws into a pond, or buries. There the ghost must stay for a thousand years, unless some foolish person frees it.

The conjuring parsons of English tradition are generally nameless and dateless, but in Europe legend-cycles developed round named clerics, ranging in time from the Middle Ages to the nineteenth century. These anecdotes, often very entertaining, circulated from one country to another and were applied to every 'master magician' in turn. Here, for instance, in a story collected in 1870, a Norwegian minister, Christian Holst (1743-1823) exorcizes the Devil in much the same way as John Schorne:

'Bring an empty whisky keg, Mother,' said the minister, for now he was angry. And when he had the keg, he started chanting and chanting, so that a shudder ran through everybody in the room. And all at once the Devil came in through the keyhole, and, whining and wagging his tail like a dog, crawled across the floor to the minister. And down in the keg he had to go. When he was well down inside, the minister popped in a cork and said, 'Well, Devil, damn you, you're mine!' Since then, they've never seen the Devil at Stor-Valle!
Reidar Th. Christiansen, *Folktales of Norway*, London and Chicago, 1964, p. 31.

Other favourite anecdotes tell how some priest got the Devil to build a bridge, promising to pay him by giving him the first living soul that crossed over it, but cheated by driving a dog or cat across; or how he saved his soul (or someone else's) from the Devil by setting him a task impossible to him, e.g. counting the letters in the Bible, which the Devil cannot bear to read.

The power of magician-priests comes from two sources: priesthood, and learnedness. Rumours were current about a secret 'Black School' of magic allegedly established in some famous, but distant, university: Wittenburg, Toledo, Paris, Cracow, Salamanca have all been suspected. A recurrent anecdote–told, for instance, about the

Icelander Saemundur the Wise (1056-1133), who really did study in Paris, as well as about Michael Scot and various Scottish lairds and Scandinavian parsons—concerns a clever pupil's escape from the Black School. All were supposed to pass together through a certain door on completing their studies, and the Devil would seize the hindmost and drag him to Hell; the clever hero saves himself, and his fellow-students, by going last but tricking the Devil into taking his shadow, or his cloak.

This link between scholarship and wizardry was strengthened by the prevalence among intellectuals from the Renaissance to the late seventeenth century of Neoplatonic systems of 'high magic', astrology, and alchemy, occupying the borderline between religion, occultism and science. To the uneducated, these sophisticated speculations seemed indistinguishable from crude magic, and equally suspect of diabolical influence; in popular traditions, scholars such as Paracelsus, Albertus Magnus, Friar Bacon and Agrippa von Nettesheim figure as wizards who made pacts with the Devil, like Faustus. So close was the presumed connection between occult powers and learning that one English writer complained in 1600, 'Nowadays among the common people a man is not adjudged any scholar at all unless he can tell men's horoscopes, cast out devils, or hath some skill in soothsaying.' Various learned medieval and Renaissance books on occultism and alchemy were translated from Latin into vernaculars. There were also popular books of spells, some of which have been in circulation from the Middle Ages to the present day—*The Key of Solomon, Le Grand Grimoire, The Sixth and Seventh Books of Moses, Cyprianus*, etc.—which claimed to be written by ancient and famous personages, but are crude, simplistic productions.

Black Magicians

All legendary magicians are credited with owning manuals of spells. Another widespread legend tells how a pupil opens his master's book and inadvertently raises a host of devils, all demanding work; the boy keeps them busy at an impossible task, such as weaving ropes of sand, till the master returns and uses his greater authority to dismiss them. This is always a light-hearted tale, but some legends see magic books as very evil. In Icelandic tradition, Bishop Gottskálk Nikulásson (1497-1520) is reputed to have been a powerful black magician whose book of spells, written in gold runes and bound in red vellum, was supposedly buried with him. Two hundred years later, a young student named Loftur is said to have been so obsessed with ambition to get this book that he used his own considerable knowledge of magic to raise Gottskálk from his grave and order him to hand it over. So terrible was the contest of wills between the dead Bishop and the living student that a terrified onlooker rang the church bell and broke Loftur's spells. The Bishop sank back into his grave, taking the book with him. Loftur, believing himself damned, drowned himself—or, some say, was drowned by the Devil. His death, which occurred in 1722 or 1723, was the kernel of truth around which the story grew.

In most countries there is someone, real or legendary, who is said to have sold his soul to obtain magic power and been carried off to Hell at last. In Poland, there is Pan Twardowski; in Rumania, Dr Salowar; in Bohemia, Dr Kittel; in the Tyrol, Pfeiffer Hinsile; in Germany, the most famous of all, Dr George (or Johann) Faustus. 'Faustus' is almost certainly a pseudonym, meaning 'lucky', but the person really existed; the first mention of him, in 1507, is an Abbot's angry denunciation of 'a vagrant, charlatan and rascal' named Georgius Sabellicus and calling himself 'Faustus Junior, fountainhead

Left. A wooden panel, c. 1500, showing John Schorne ordering the Devil to get into a boot. Schorne is also said to have resurrected a dead ox, and made a well by striking the ground with his staff during a drought. The Rector and Churchwardens of St Gregory's Sudbury, Suffolk, on loan to Gainsborough's House, Sudbury.

Right. The legend of Theophilus. Furious at not having been made Abbot, the monk Theophilus swore allegiance to Satan and made a pact with him; later he repented and was saved by the Virgin Mary. Musée Condé, Chantilly.

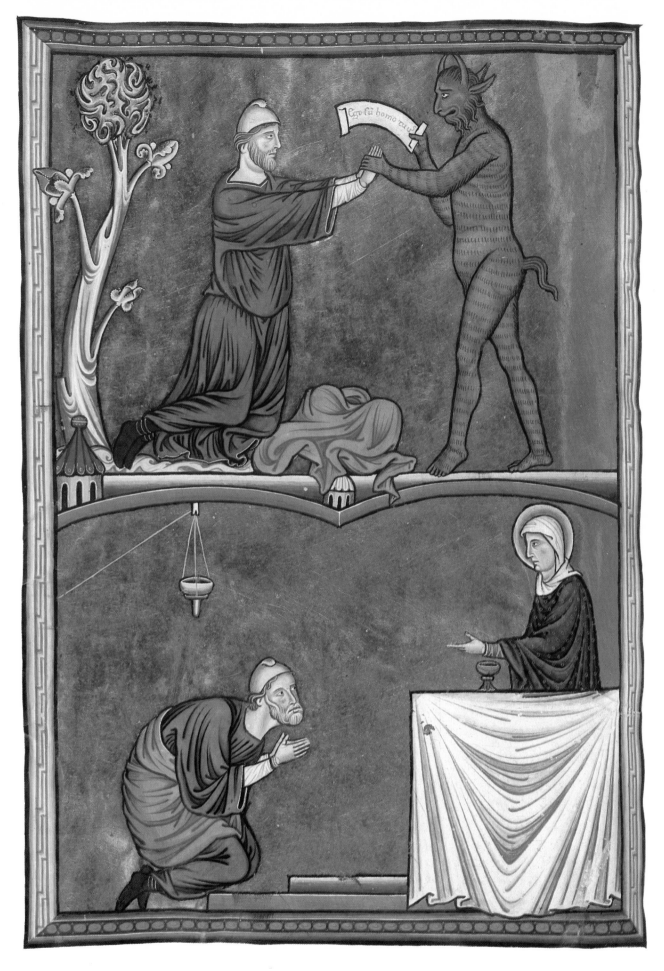

of necromancers, astrologers, second Magus', currently publicizing himself as skilled in occult arts. The title 'Faustus *Junior*' must imply that Sabellicus was exploiting the fame of some previous magician of the same name, but who this was is now unknown. Sabellicus/Faustus himself, however, can be traced in various German towns between 1513 and 1537; he practised medicine, palmistry, crystal-gazing, astrology, necromancy, and fortune-telling. He was often protected by aristocratic patrons, and presumably most of his clients were satisfied, though some contemporaries called him a swindler. He died in 1539 or 1540.

The blackening of his reputation soon began. Writing in 1544, the theologian Johann Gast claimed that when he supped with Faustus at Basel he saw him attended by a dog and a horse which were obviously demons;

Gast also declared that the Devil strangled Faustus, and that his corpse persistently turned to lie face downwards on the bier, though it was righted five times. Legends multiplied, and in 1587 appeared a sensational chapbook giving Faustus's life-story in the form which has been familiar ever since. It recounts his pact with Mephistopheles, signed in blood; the twenty-four years of wonder-working; the raising of the ghost of Helen of Troy; Faust's panic and vain remorse as the appointed hour approaches, and his hideous death:

At midnight a fearful storm arose; horrible hisses as of a thousand serpents were heard, and for a little the agonizing cries of Faust, with a hollow and suffocating sound; but soon all was still. In the morning the floor of the room was found stained with blood, the brains were spattered on the walls, and his body was found outside, lying near a dunghill, the head and every member hanging half torn off.
Chambers Encyclopedia, London, 1930, under 'Faust'.

The central section of this *Faustbuch* contains adventurous episodes, some farcical, as when Faust makes stag's horns grow on the Emperor's courtiers' heads, and invisibly disrupts the Pope's banquet. His servant Wagner is also comical. The general tone, however, is grim, with many admonitions about the damnable consequences of magic and trafficking with Satan. The booklet was an instant success, soon widely translated; the English version, which inspired Marlowe's play, dates from 1589. At the popular level, it was adapted into a puppet play which was still seen at German fairs, like a Punch and Judy

Frontispiece to Thomas Heywood's *Merlin's Prophecies and Predictions Interpreted* (1651). Merlin, represented as a monk (perhaps by confusion with medieval clerical 'magicians' such as Friar Bacon), holds a book entitled 'The Red Dragon'. In the background are the beasts used constantly as symbols in the obscure language of prophecies: dragons, a lion, a bear, a unicorn, etc.

show, early in the present century. On the literary level, Faust's legend inspired masterpieces by Marlowe, Goethe and Thomas Mann.

Poets as Magicians and Seers

A learned skill more ancient than any taught in medieval universities is the skill of poetry, so it is understandable that in many cultures poets were sometimes regarded as having magical powers; spells, after all, usually required accurate memorization, and resembled verse by their verbal patterning and rhythmic recitation. It was thought that a poet's words, if directed by hostile intent, had devastating physical effects; medieval Irish and Icelandic traditions describe 'satirists' (i.e. composers of abusive or cursing verses) who inflicted boils, baldness or impotence on their enemies; in later folklore, there are tales about versifiers who could lay ghosts and kill vermin, especially the Icelandic *kraptaskáldar*, 'poets of power'.

Some famous legendary magicians were also poets, notably Taliesin and Merlin. Taliesin, court poet to a sixth-century Welsh chieftain, was remembered as an outstanding bard; by the sixteenth century he was the hero of various dramatic magical adventures, the best known being about how he won his powers. He was originally a boy called Gwion, servant to a witch, who one day accidentally tasted a brew he was meant to be guarding. The witch tried to kill him; he fled, changing into various animal shapes, but still pursued by her in shapes of corresponding predators, till he turned into a grain of wheat and she into a hen, which swallowed him. This was her undoing; he entered her womb and was reborn as a preternaturally wise baby named Taliesin, 'Fair Brow'. As an adult, he is said to have served his prince as a seer. Versified 'prophecies' played an important role in political propaganda in medieval Wales, and were generally fathered onto some ancient and authoritative figure; Taliesin's name was often used in this way, as was the even more famous name of Merlin.

Merlin (Welsh Myrddin) lived–if he really existed, which is uncertain–around 600 A.D. in the Welsh-speaking region of Lowland Scotland. According to the earliest accounts, he was a poet who ran mad when the king he served was killed in a battle in 573 A.D.; from then on he lived as a wild man in the forests, uttering prophecies of doom. The association of madness with supernatural power is a Celtic commonplace; there is an Irish parallel to this aspect of Merlin's career in the tale of Suibhne Galt ('Mad Sweeney') who was crazed

Abriß eines pfiffers so sich vff ein zeit
ano 1 2 8 4 Zue Hamelen an der Weser
erzaigt vnd befunden hatt Jm Braunschweig

Die Statt
Hamelen
Jn Braunschwig

Weser

by panic in battle and flew from tree to tree like a bird. A Scottish madman of the same type, Lailoken, is mentioned in the eighth-century *Life of St Kentigern*, and in some texts is identified with Merlin.

In none of these early references is Merlin linked to Arthur. This link, which was crucial to the spread of his fame, had occurred by the twelfth century and was incorporated into the influential writings of Geoffrey of Monmouth. Geoffrey knew and used the old legend of the mad forest-dwelling Merlin, but he gave far more prominence to other themes: Merlin as a marvelously wise boy, begotten by a demon on a nun; as the builder of Stonehenge; as the wise counsellor of Uther Pendragon, and later of his son Arthur. Other medieval authors took up these ideas, stressing particularly Merlin's role as a venerable sage, the guiding genius of Arthur's reign; his 'primitive' madness was eliminated, and his prophecies became little more than wise warnings given to Arthur. In this form, the legend of Merlin entered the mainstream of European romantic literature.

In England and Wales, however, Merlin was still significant in popular tradition as the alleged author of various obscure 'prophecies' with political overtones, which circulated, with constantly updated interpre-

York and Lancaster. In *Henry IV*, Shakespeare mocks Owen Glendower's belief in 'the dreamer Merlin and his prophecies' about moles and ants and dragons, 'A clip-winged griffin and a moulting raven/And such a deal of skimble-skamble stuff...' There is also a glancing allusion to Merlin's prophecies in *King Lear*; clearly the topic was a familiar one to Elizabethan audiences.

In the Middle Ages, Virgil too was regarded as a great magus, whose learning enabled him to perform marvels through occult arts. The Church hailed him as an inspired prophet, since his *Fourth Eclogue* was by then interpreted as foretelling Christ's birth; readers of the *Aeneid* also regarded his description of Hades with awe–this was one reason why he was an appropriate guide for Dante's Otherworld journey. Meanwhile, popular legends in Italy presented him as a benevolent inventor of magic talismans to protect his birthplace, Naples. According to these tales (first recorded in 1114), Virgil had built a model of the city, and Naples would remain safe so long as this model remained hidden and undamaged; he had made a bronze statue to prevent Vesuvius from erupting, and a bronze fly to chase all flies away; he had rounded up all the snakes in Naples and imprisoned them underground; he had made baths that cured all diseases. His body, secretly buried in a cavern or a sea-girt castle, was a powerful protector; to remove it would bring disaster. The twelfth-century sources say he accomplished all this simply by 'incantations' and 'mathematic art', but later writers say he learned magic from a host of demons whom he released from a glass bottle. With the coming of printing the Virgil

legends, like those of Faust, became widely known; but unlike Faust, Virgil remained essentially a white magician, who might command demons but made no pact with them, and used his power for useful ends and to punish the wicked.

The Secret Skills of Craftsmen

The prestige of 'book-learned' men, whether priests, scholars or poets, had an equivalent among the non-literate in the mystique surrounding certain specialist crafts, especially those involving mastery over animals. They were taught by a long, secretive personal training, by older worker to apprentice (often by father to son), and an aura of mystery was deliberately fostered to impress outsiders; expertise might be ascribed to innate hereditary abilities, or even to supernatural assistance from fairies or demons. There are interesting near-contemporary examples from rural Hungary, where ancient customs and beliefs remained undisturbed up to the Second World War. There, particular mystique lent prestige to herdsmen and shepherds, who spent much of the year apart from other farm serfs, pasturing their animals in remote regions. The job usually passed from father to son, together with much esoteric lore concerning the control of animals, cures for their ailments, spells to keep wolves and evil spirits away, charms to improve the yield of milk and wool, and so forth. Descendants of famous herdsmen boasted of their powers. Some, it was said, used to scare wolves away by playing a pipe of wolf-bone, or simply by calling them 'Nice lambs!' and threatening to take their pelts for a fur coat. Others could order dogs, or even bulls, to run errands for them, or had magic ways of immobilizing a flock:

There was a shepherd in Hortobágy who drove his stick into the ground next to the flock and then the sheep didn't go away. Another drove his stick into the ground, put his long embroidered felt coat and his hat on it, and went to an inn drinking. He returned only late in the night, but the stick, the hat and the coat watched the flock meanwhile.
Béla Gunda, 'Magical Watching of

tations, in the medieval and Tudor periods. This reputation was largely based on enigmatic verses which Geoffrey of Monmouth had quoted (or composed?), consisting mainly of mysterious allusions to conflicts between semi-heraldic beasts such as 'the Boar of Cornwall', 'the Evil Ass', 'the Cock of the North'. Simultaneously vague and adaptable, they were repeatedly used as propaganda in the struggles between Welsh and English, English and Scots,

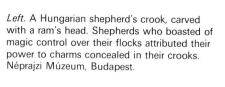

the Flock on the Great Hungarian Plain', *Folklore* 81, 1970, p. 287.

The magic of such a stick was ascribed to a snakeskin wrapped round it, or a coffin nail blessed and driven into it, or a live bee stolen at midnight on St George's Day and sealed into a hole in it. If a woman touched the stick, its power would turn awry, and the flock would scatter. Herdsmen also circled their flocks three or seven times at dusk to keep them in one place, or fumigated the pasture ground with incense, wolf's hair, or rags from a virgin's smock. These secrets were jealously guarded. Highly skilful men were said to be helped by devils, and many tales were told of contests of magic power between rival herdsmen.

Coachmen on the large Hungarian estates enjoyed a similar reputation for esoteric knowledge, being allegedly able to keep horses perfectly groomed without effort, halt them immovably by magic means, change bales of straw into horses, or revive dead horses. Some claimed their power resided in a magic whip, obtained by keeping vigil at a crossroads, despite terrifying visions and supernatural assaults. Others denied that they used demonic aid; their secret recipe was simply to catch the first red-winged butterfly of spring and squeeze its body into a crack in the coach.

At the other end of Europe, in Scotland and East Anglia, it was said that there were mysterious ways of controlling farm horses, taught by a secret fraternity known as the Society of the Horseman's Word, which existed until the First World War in parts of Scotland. This Society passed on its knowledge under oath of secrecy, after an initiation reminiscent of Freemasonry. What exactly the knowledge was remains obscure; there were rumours about magic words used in taming wild horses, or to fix a horse immovably where he stood, and about the supernatural powers of a frog's bone. A Suffolk farmworker told George Ewart Evans in the 1950s:

You get a frog and take it to a running stream at midnight, but before this you have killed it and pounded it up. You throw it into the water, and some of it will flow downstream, but a part of it—a bone—will float upstream. This is the part you have to keep.

G. Ewart Evans, *The Horse in the Furrow*, London, 1960, p. 247.

Behind this non-rational ritual procedure lay the real secret, patiently unravelled by Ewart Evans, which depended on the horses' keen awareness of scents undetectable by human noses. The old horsemen used aromatic oils rubbed into their hands or a handkerchief to 'draw' a horse to them; conversely, no horse would pass a gatepost, say, on which noxious-smelling substances had secretly been smeared. The frog-bones, Evans showed, were not used alone, but combined with scented oils, and probably had a scent of their own, since they had been steeped in herbs and chemicals to 'cure' them. How far the horsemen themselves believed in the magic efficacy of the bone and the dramatic nocturnal ritual involved in obtaining it, is unclear. Some may genuinely have believed in it, while others only mentioned it to mystify

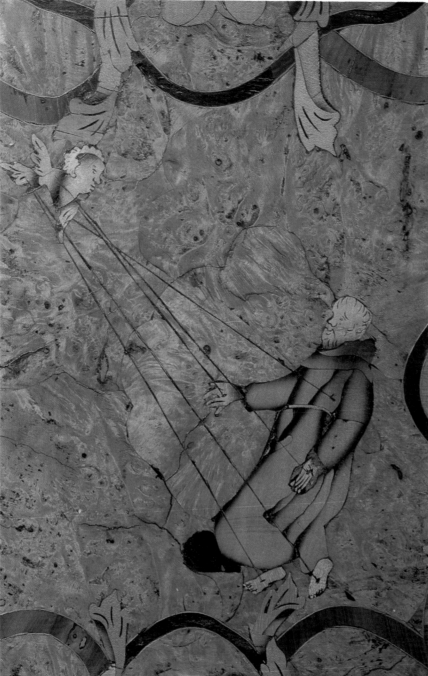

Iceland, for instance, it is said that long ago a wizard lured every mouse on the Akureyjar Isles into a pit by the smell of a roast leg of mutton, and had the pit filled in; from then on, there were no mice there, until years later careless workmen reopened the pit and let them all out, since when they have been a pest on the islands. In Ireland, it was commonly said that plagues of rats could be stopped if a poet laid a paper bearing a written charm near their hole; one rat would emerge and seize the paper in his jaws, and then lead all the rest away to whatever place had been named in the charm–generally the home of someone the poet disliked. In Norwegian tradition, Laplanders, who are credited with many occult skills, are said to destroy snakes magically; one widespread tale tells how a Lappish wizard drew all the snakes of a district into a bonfire by the power of his chants, till there came a *Linnorm* (a sort of dragon, sixteen and a half yards long) which, though compelled to enter the flames like the rest, dragged the wizard with it, so that man and monster perished together.

Even nowadays, holy men are sometimes assumed to be able to banish pests. On 5 May 1924, some pilgrims were on their way to an Italian monastery to visit a famous saintly priest, Padre Pio, when they came to a road totally covered with masses of black caterpillars. A man from the monastery explained that these creatures had infested an almond tree whose owner, desperate at the damage to his crop, begged Padre Pio to bless the tree. He did, and within a few minutes the whole swarm set off down the street. The gulf between a saint and a magician, so wide in theory, is in practice often all too narrow.

outsiders, conceal the importance of the smelly oils, and enhance their own prestige as masters of occult powers.

Even the rat-catcher's humble calling had its mystique, with traditions about men who summoned and dismissed rodents by magical authority. By far the best known is the tale of the Pied Piper of Hamlyn, who first cleared the town of a plague of rats but then, when payment was refused, lured all its children into a hollow mountain. This is alleged to have happened on 26 June 1284. The story was first recorded in 1370, almost a hundred years later; the earliest versions do not mention rats or rat-catchers, merely saying that 'someone' marched away with 150 children–it is only in 1557 that this person is identified as a rat-catcher. Various rationalizations have been proposed, for instance that the children were lured away on a so-called Crusade by an itinerant preacher, but concrete evidence is lacking.

Whatever may have happened at Hamlyn, the motif of a magician driving vermin away is fairly widespread. In

Shape-changing and Witchcraft

The Superhuman Powers of Evil

Belief in witches, and in such related concepts as the power of the Evil Eye and the ability of certain persons to change into animal form, has had an enormous role in folk tradition, and in many areas of Europe survives to this day more strongly than, say, the belief in fairies. Psychologically this is understandable, for its enduring function is to supply an explanation, and a scapegoat, for personal misfortunes, disease, crop failure, loss of livestock, and the like. Its great advantage is that it offers a permissible focus for anger. If one thinks misfortune comes from God, one must bear it humbly; if from fairies or demons, one can protect oneself by charms, but there is no way to retaliate; but if the evil comes from a human agent, a fellow-member of the community, he or she can be identified and punished. At one level, the witch is thought of as a more or less normal person whose hostile actions, though magical in their effects, are not in themselves outside human capacities; she may work by cursing, for example, by a hypnotic glance, or by sticking pins into a doll. At another level, however, the witch is a topic for fantasies of hate and fear; the supernatural powers ascribed to her are so abnormal that her human identity becomes obscured and her image merges with that of female demons and ogresses. She is said to turn into an animal at will; to enter houses invisibly; to ride through the air on various objects; to eat children, or suck their blood; to feed upon the strength of her victims. Such sinister and impossible beliefs constitute the 'mythology' of witchcraft, transforming each suspected village woman into a stereotype of supernatural evil; they are notorious now for their role in the witch-hunts which swept Europe from about 1450 till roughly 1700, but their roots are far older, and they persist in folk legends to this day.

One of the oldest and most widespread is the belief that some people can turn themselves into animals. In non-Christian cultures, this is by no means always seen as an evil activity; on the contrary, Arctic shamans are often said to send out their souls to the Otherworld in animal form (their bodies meanwhile lying in trance) in order to rescue the souls of the sick or to obtain useful information from spirits. Good and evil shamans might encounter and fight one another during these spirit journeys; according to traditions gathered by Christian missionaries, Lappish magicians were thought to fight as reindeer. An elaborated version of a shapechanger's battle is found in certain fairytales and similar entertaining folk-fictions, for instance in a fourteenth-century Icelandic saga (*Sturlaugs saga starfsama*), describing a contest between a youth and a Lapp wizard. First they fought in their natural shapes, but then suddenly they vanished, 'and in their place were two dogs, biting one another furiously'; these vanished too, and onlookers saw two eagles tearing at each other in mid-air, till one fell dead and the other flew away. The story of Taliesin fleeing from the witch Ceridwen (above, p. 93) is a variation on this theme in which he, seemingly the weaker, is swallowed by his enemy, yet triumphs in the end by exploiting her femininity.

In modern Europe, it is only in Hungary that this archaic theme still commands some measure of belief. There, it is traditionally believed that a boy born with teeth showing, or with extra fingers, will grow up to be a

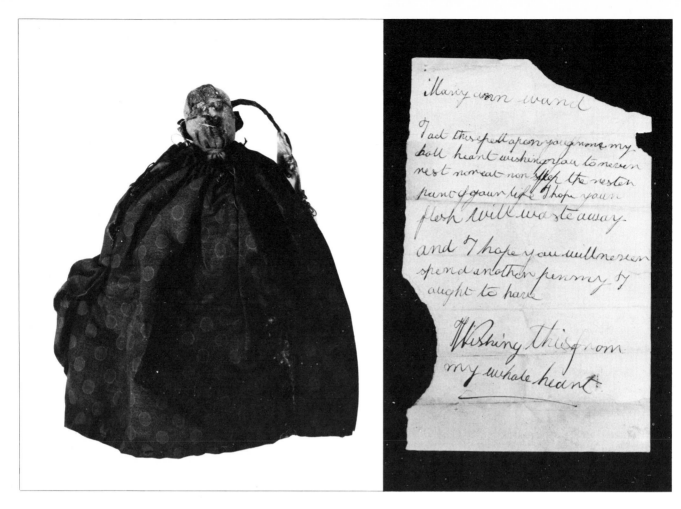

garabonciás, a benevolent wizard; in his seventh or fourteenth year he will test his powers by fighting an elder wizard in animal form. A tale recorded in 1959 describes such a battle:

The boy drank the water in the trough, and then he shook himself, and all at once he turned into a bull. A bull of leaden-white colour. Uncle Peter walked round him in great amazement. 'Oh, sonny, what a strange thing to happen!'

Suddenly, he sees a big cloud coming on. And next thing, it comes down, right in front of them. And as soon as it comes down, a black, sooty-necked bull steps out of it. And in a rage it goes kicking up the earth with its hoofs and tossing it sky-high with its horns. And there it goes, straight for the white bull. And they charge against one another, and in what fury they butt each other! Not under the sun has there ever been such a fight between two bulls.
Linda Dégh, p. 274.

In medieval Icelandic writings, the balance is beginning to change. There are still some 'good' shapechangers, though mostly they are figures from remote heroic ages, closely linked to mythology–the hero Bothvar Bjarki, for instance, doing battle as a bear, and the Volsung heroes Sigmund and Sinfjotli living for a while as werewolves. Usually, however, saga shapechangers are evil witches and wizards, and are supposedly members of normal communities in a comparatively recent past. Thus in *Kormaks saga*, which is about a tenth-century Icelandic poet, there is a witch who appears as a walrus, though still recognizable by her human eyes, and tries to capsize Kormak's boat; when he strikes the walrus, Thordis herself receives the wound.

This is an early example of a recurrent motif in witch-beliefs: a witch is wounded while in animal form, and later a corresponding wound is noticed on her own body, thus proving her guilt. As Gervase of Tilbury states in his *Otia Imperialia* (*c.* 1211): 'Women have been

seen and wounded in the shape of cats by persons who were secretly on the watch, and . . . next day the women have shown wounds and loss of limbs.' A British variant, extremely common in nineteenth-century folklore collections, tells how huntsmen repeatedly sighted a hare but failed to catch it, because it always disappeared near a certain old woman's house. If they knocked at the door, they would find her in her chair, panting. Eventually a hound managed to bite the hare's rump as it fled, and when next seen, the old woman had a wounded leg. At English witch trials in the sixteenth and seventeenth centuries, such anecdotes were sometimes seriously proffered in evidence. At that of Julia Cox at Taunton in 1663 one witness claimed that an exhausted hare he had been chasing collapsed beside a bush and turned into the accused woman before his very eyes; when he asked her what she was doing there, 'she was so far out of breath that she could not make him any answer.' Edward Fairfax wrote in his *Daemonologia*

Left. This doll was found in 1960 hidden in a cellar in a house in Hereford, with a written curse pinned to its skirt; it probably dates from the eighteenth century. Home-made magic was a way of seeking vengeance for one's grudges. Hereford City Museum.

Right. In the early Middle Ages, the Church taught that alleged flights by witches were mere delusions. By the fifteenth century it had reversed its position and accepted that magic flights, animal transformations, and Sabbats were realities, achieved by Satan's power. Woodcut from Ulrich Molitor, *De Lariis et Phitonicis Mulieribus* (1490).

(1622) that 'The changing of witches into hares, cats and the like shapes is so common, as late testimonies and confessions approve unto us, that none but the stupidly incredulous can wrong the credit of the reporters or doubt of the certainty.'

Werewolves and Nightmares

Shapechanging is only one among many elements in the stereotype of a witch, but it is the essence of werewolves, which were believed in in most parts of Europe, and were already well known to the Romans. Virgil's *Eighth Eclogue* describes a sorcerer who turned himself into a wolf with poisonous herbs. Petronius includes in his *Satyricon* an anecdote about a *versipellis* ('turnskin') who was wounded as a wolf and showed the corresponding wound in his human body; this story is supposedly told by an ex-slave, presumably reflecting a belief current among the uneducated but ludicrous to the upper classes. In Christian times, however, learned men were just as ready as the

peasants to credit the existence of werewolves, whose powers they ascribed to the Devil's intervention, though they differed as to what exactly occurred. The matter was much debated in the sixteenth century, when many men were tried for murders allegedly committed while in wolf form. Some lawyers and scholars believed in literal, physical transformation achieved by the Devil's help; others, that the man fell into a trance while his soul entered into and controlled the body of a real wolf; others, that the Devil bewitched the man so that he seemed, both to himself and to others, to be a wolf, but that this was sheer delusion. All, however, agreed that the man was fully to blame, having become a werewolf by a deliberate pact with Satan, with murderous intent.

In folk tradition, in contrast, the werewolf is frequently envisaged as an unwilling or even unconscious victim of some curse, spell, ill-luck, or freak of nature; all sorts of reasons are given to explain why men become werewolves,

without any diabolical pact. Sometimes, it is said to be a punishment visited on a child for its parents' sexual sins. In the Périgord region of France, it was thought that priests' bastards grew up as werewolves; legends collected in Romania in 1975 attribute the condition to the child having been conceived on Christmas Eve or Easter Saturday (it being sinful to have sexual intercourse on the fast days preceding major feasts), or to his being born on Easter Sunday. Such babies, it is thought, have animal traits such as a harelip or 'wolf-eyes', and hate humanity because of their anger at their parents' sin. Alternatively, the mother alone may be to blame, because she tried to avoid the pains of childbirth and of breast-feeding, which were allotted to her by God; thus, Romanians hold that if a woman refuses to breastfeed her child it grows up into a werewolf, or turns permanently into a wild beast. A Swedish informant in 1915 gave this explanation for werewolves and their female equivalents, the 'nightmares':

It happened to people because their mothers had taken the membranes from newborn foals. They put it up on stakes and ran naked under it three times while they were pregnant. If they did that, they were supposed to have an easy labour and a painless delivery. But if they did it, it would affect the unborn child. If it was a girl it would become a nightmare; if it was a boy it would become a werewolf. The nightmare usually takes the form of an invisible little thing that can go through keyholes and cover people's mouths while they lie asleep. . . . There are still people who believe in that today.
John Lindow, p. 176.

Other explanations for involuntary werewolves include, in various countries, that they had unwittingly picked a certain plant or drunk from a certain stream which could produce the transformation; or put on a belt of wolfskin, deliberately or accidentally; or been cursed by a magician; or were affected by the moon. Gervase of Tilbury claims: 'In England we often see men changed into wolves at the changes of the moon, which kind of men the French call *gerulfos*, but the English *werewulf*.'

The degree to which werewolves were feared varies correspondingly. In medieval romances, they are innocent victims, sympathetically portrayed; in modern Romania they are pitied as tragic, and their potential danger to the community can be prevented by simple magical precautions. At some periods,

however, notably in late sixteenth-century France, men were tried and executed for murdering (and sometimes partly eating) children, while in wolf guise. They were accused of making pacts with the Devil and transforming themselves with magic ointments, but presumably they were just psychopathic multiple murderers, possibly suffering from delusions that they could become wolves. Interestingly, surviving recipes for the ointments allegedly used by both werewolves and witches often include hallucinogenic herbs such as aconite, belladonna, hemlock and poppy, which might be absorbed through the skin; anyone expecting to experience the sensation of transformation might well obtain it by this means. Whatever the reason, the accused men confessed both

to the murders and to the shapechanging, and were duly put to death.

The Scandinavian werewolf was regarded as dangerous to pregnant women because his nature impelled him to rip the foetus from their wombs. However, he might be disenchanted simply by being recognized, as in this Norwegian story about a were-bear:

There was a strange belief in the old days that some people, at times, had to take on a bear-hide. There was something about them that was under a spell. In Fäarland, in Sogn, there was once such a man-bear. One time, when his wife was with child, he said to her: 'Now I have to go away for a while. If a bear should come to you while I am gone, throw your apron at it, and run away.'

A while later, sure enough, a bear did come and attack her, and she did as her man had said and got away. When the man came home and sat down to eat, he started picking shreds of cloth out of his teeth, and his wife saw that they were shreds of her apron. Since it had now been discovered, he was freed from the spell, and was not a man-bear any longer.

Reidar Th. Christiansen, *Folktales of Norway*, pp. 48-9.

The nightmare or *mara* resembles the werewolf in being a normal person by day and a preternatural being by night; throughout Germany and Scandinavia she was said to enter houses invisibly and crouch on sleepers' chests, choking them and causing them nightmares, and also to exhaust horses and cattle by riding them at night, without being aware of what she was doing. This unawareness distinguishes her from witches, whose 'night-riding' of humans and animals was deliberately malevolent. When trapped, the *mara* generally loses her powers and regains her health, having previously felt chronically tired and sick; in some stories, however, she is wounded or killed while in her preternatural state, just like a shapechanging witch.

Involuntary shapechanging also figures among the present-day folk beliefs of Sardinian shepherds, who think a man can sometimes become possessed

by a monstrous ox-spirit, which itself is animated by ghosts of former suicides. The victim seems normal by day, but by night his soul leaves his sleeping body and becomes an ox, laden with chains; in this form he roams the village, hideously bellowing outside the house of anyone destined for disaster or death. Before dawn he returns to his body, unaware of what he has been doing.

Night-flying Witches

Besides animal transformations, the 'mythological' stereotype of the witch constantly draws upon two other sinister themes: the ability to fly or ride through the air, and cannibalism. All three are combined in the Roman *strix* or 'screecher', described by Pliny, Ovid, Petronius, Apuleius and others. A *strix* was a ravenous owl-like bird, or rather a woman in the form of this bird, which either ripped open babies' bellies to eat their entrails, or killed them by offering them its own poisonous breasts to suck; it also magically sucked out the strength and virility of living men. In Jewish demonology much the same is said about Lilith. She strangles newborn babies, or sucks their blood and marrow, and endangers women in childbirth; she seduces sleeping men, whose nocturnal emissions beget her hosts of demonic offspring, who fly with her by night. Sometimes it is said that she was 'the first Eve', created at the same time as Adam, but flew away and became a demon rather than submit to his masculine authority.

In early medieval Europe the theme emerges clearly in a series of questions devised by Bishop Burchard of Worms around 1008-12, for priests to use when interrogating penitents about their superstitions:

Have you believed . . . that in the silence of the quiet night, when you have settled down in bed . . . you are able to go out through closed doors and travel the world with others similarly deceived; and that without visible weapons you kill people . . . and together cook and devour their flesh; and that where the heart was, you put straw or wood; and that after eating these people, you bring them alive and grant them a brief spell of life?

If you have believed this, you shall do penance on bread and water for fifty days, and likewise in each of the seven years following.

Quoted in Norman Cohn, *Europe's Inner Demons*, London and New York, 1975, p. 209.

This shows that the fantasy about cannibalistic night-flying witches was so ingrained in German peasant communities that some women believed themselves to be acting it out; the Church, however, at this stage, rejected their belief and punished them for it, though the penance is, by medieval standards, a mild one. Another medieval document, the *Canon Episcopi* (c. 906), is equally scathing about another group of women who imagine they travel magically in company with some female supernatural being, whom the

clerical writer equates with the Roman goddess Diana:

Some wicked women, perverted by Satan and led astray by illusions and fantasies induced by demons, believe that they ride out at night on beasts with Diana, the pagan goddess, and a great multitude of women, and that in the silence of the night they cross many vast regions. . . . It is only the mind that does all this, but people who lack the true faith believe that these things happen physically too. Colin, p. 211.

Since there is no mention here of cannibalism or magic murder, the 'Diana' round whom these women's fantasies centred must have been a benevolent figure, not a witch. Interestingly, when Burchard of Worms quoted this passage a hundred years later, he equated 'Diana' with Holda, a figure in German folklore who is on the whole kindly and protective. Holda is said to visit farmsteads during the midwinter nights, to see if they are well kept; ploughs, crops, spinning and weaving are all under her patronage; like Father Christmas, she brings gifts for children. However, like the Austrian Bertha/Perchta, whom she closely resembles, she may also lead the terrifying Wild Hunt (pp. 41, 44-5), and may appear as an ugly hag to punish naughty children (pp. 65, 128). Presumably Burchard had some reason to think that the women mentioned in the *Canon Episcopi* imagined themselves to be accompanying Holda on her nocturnal visitations. Another interesting detail in the *Canon Episcopi* is the riding upon beasts, which foreshadows the interest of later accounts of witchcraft in the weird modes of transport for going to the sabbat: real horses, cats or goats; phantom horses created by magic from straws or twigs; human beings metamorphosed into horses; broomsticks, pitchforks, hurdles, stools and so on, rubbed with magic ointment to make them fly.

Murdering children was an atrocity commonly attributed to witches; they were said to eat them at a ritual feast at the sabbat, or boil them to make magic ointments from their fat. These crimes were supposedly enacted on a psychic level, as Burchard's words make clear; the victim thus 'eaten' would have still 'a brief spell of life' before falling sick and dying. Similar gruesome fantasies had long formed part of the stereotype image of secret religious societies, as imagined by their enemies. Romans had thought Christians held secret meetings to drink the blood of babies, mixed with the ashes of their burned corpses. Christians made comparable accusations against many heretics: against Paulicians in the early eighth century, a sect at Orleans in 1022, Waldensians from the thirteenth to the fifteenth centuries, a splinter-group of Franciscans called Fraticelli in 1466. These groups, and others, were also thought to hold sexual orgies and worship the Devil – all notions which were gradually combined and transferred to witches, to build up the standard picture of a sabbat. This stereotype was formalized by theologians and church lawyers, culminating in such works as the notorious *Malleus Maleficarum* (1486), providing guidance for the intensive questioning of suspects during the great witch-hunts, whereby numerous con-

fessions were sought and obtained. Public panic and suspicion must have been intense. Nevertheless, the alleged cannibalism and murders remained firmly in the psychic sphere; no real corpses of murdered children figured in witch-trials—unlike trials of were-wolves, which were often precipitated by outbreaks of multiple murder and/or killings by real wolves. Those who claimed to be bewitched were suffering from normal diseases, even if they were convinced they were being 'eaten', like the wife of the parson of St Osyth (Essex) in 1582, who cried out on her deathbed 'Oh Annis Herd, Annis Herd, she hath consumed me!'

Familiars

Another 'mythological' motif, particularly common in Britain, was that witches possessed familiars—evil spirits, generally in the shape of small animals, given them by the Devil or an older witch—and allowed them to suck their blood. These creatures ran errands for them, bringing sickness and misfortune to their enemies. British witch-trials often mention familiars, usually realistically: a cat, dog, toad, mouse, weasel or bird is seen in the suspect's house, or a fly enters her prison, and witnesses claim that this is her familiar. English folk-legends are equally sober; one of the few sensational traits they ascribe to the animal familiar is that the witch is supposedly unable to die until she has bequeathed it to someone else.

In Finland and Sweden, however, there is a far more extraordinary familiar, the 'milk-hare' or 'carrier', first attested in wall-paintings of the mid-fifteenth century, and subsequently mentioned in many oral and written sources. Usually it looks like a rabbit or hare, but it has been created by the witch from normal household objects—knitting needles, a spindle wrapped in wool, a stocking, a knot of nine different wools—which she has brought to life with a drop of her own blood, while reciting some such formula as:

So long as you will run for me,
I will burn in Hell for thee.

The creature would run among the cows of the witch's neighbours, sucking their milk, and return to spew the stolen milk into her churn. In Iceland, where witchcraft traditions are particularly macabre, the beliefs about the 'carrier' were summarized thus by the folklorist Jón Árnason in 1864:

To get a Carrier, a woman must steal a dead man's rib from the churchyard on Whitsun morning, soon after he has been buried; then she wraps it in grey woollen yarn which she has stolen elsewhere . . ., wrapping it round the rib till it looks like a hank of wool, and this she keeps between her breasts for a while. Afterwards, she goes three times to Communion, and each time she lets the Wine (or, some say, both Bread and Wine) dribble onto the materials which will form the Carrier, by spitting it into her bosom. . . . The first time the woman dribbles onto the Carrier, it lies quite still; the second time, it stirs; the third time, it is so strong and lively that it tries to jump out of her bosom. . . . Then she draws blood from the inside of her thigh, which causes a fleshy growth there, and she lets it suck there. It lives there and feeds on the woman's blood whenever it is at home, and therefore one can always recognise those who are 'Carriers' Mothers' because they are lame and have blood-red warts inside their thighs.

Jacqueline Simpson, *The Folktales and Legends of Iceland*, London, 1972, p. 180.

Other gruesome and fantastic magic recipes from Iceland include a 'Witch-Bridle', made from the skin and bones of a freshly buried corpse; when this is laid across any man, beast, or object, it will rise into the air and carry the witch wherever she wants. Then there are 'Money Breeches' made by flaying a corpse in one piece from the waist down; whoever wears them always has money in his pocket, but if he dies before stripping them off and giving them to someone else, he will be damned.

The Wizard's Slave

Above all, Iceland has rich traditions about necromancy. Wizards were thought to raise corpses from their graves and 'put strength' into them; they were called 'Sendings', for wizards sent them to attack their enemies. The 'Sending' was often non-material in its manifestations (for instance, it could be invisible, or change into animal form), but it invariably originated as a corpse, or, at the least, as a particular bone from a corpse, usually a vertebra. It presents a curious blend of archaic concepts and learned theories. The major source is undoubtedly the ancient Nordic belief in the *draugr*, the 'living corpse' (pp. 46-7), but there also seems to be some influence from a theological doctrine current in the sixteenth and

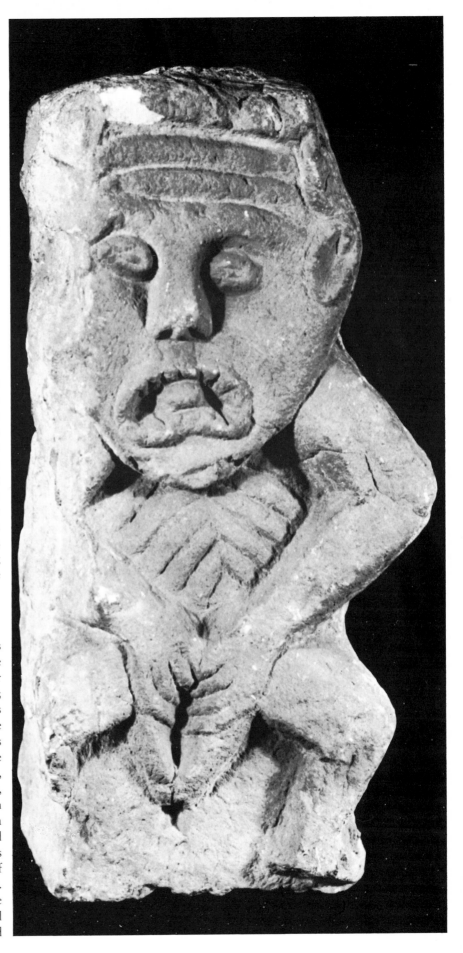

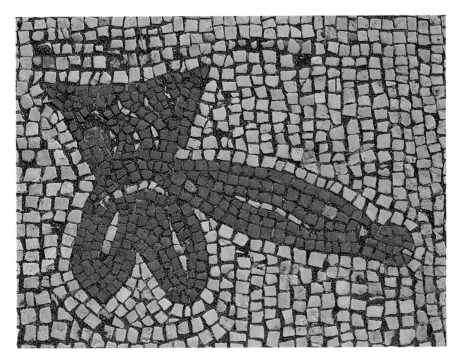

seventeenth centuries that every human skeleton contained one 'incorruptible bone' which would resist decay and form the nucleus of the soul's new body at the General Resurrection. Nineteenth-century Icelanders held that if one stabbed at a Sending and were lucky enough to strike this one bone, the creature would be defeated and destroyed, though the bone would remain. Many tales about Sendings also stress the dangers and horrors involved in raising them; a necromancer must summon the corpse from its grave by degrees, lick away the froth from its nose and mouth, and feed it with a drop of his blood. As it springs to life he must immediately wrestle with it and subdue it, or it will drag him into the grave forever. From then on, he must keep it busy, or it may turn its malevolence against its master.

Somewhat akin to the Sending, but not necessarily evil, is the animated image or pseudo-man supposedly created by some wizard to serve him. The most interesting instances are found in Jewish traditions about the *golem* (literally, 'embryo'). The term properly belongs to the symbolic language of Kabbalistic mysticism, as found in Hasidic writings of the twelfth and thirteenth centuries, where it apparently denotes a spiritual experience created by uttering sacred chants. In popular tales, however, the *golem* was

imagined to be an actual pseudo-man, created by magic, which would be at the service of the magician who had made it. Such stories began among German Jews in the fifteenth century, and soon became connected with various eminent rabbis, such as Eliph of Chelm (d. 1583). The most famous versions concern Rabbi Loew of Prague, who lived in the sixteenth century, though these stories apparently only came to be told about him some 200 years later.

A *golem* is fashioned out of dust, and brought to life by placing a paper with a sacred word on it in its mouth or round its neck. Despite the good intentions of its maker, a *golem* grows stronger every day, and is likely to become dangerous; eventually it will turn against its master and destroy him, unless it is reduced back into dust by removing the sacred word. The earlier treatments of the theme stress the *golem*'s destructive potentialities, and warn that although to make one is not in itself an act of evil sorcery, the physical and spiritual dangers outweigh the advantages. In more recent nineteenth- and twentieth-century versions, stories about the *golem* present him more as the secret champion and protector of Jews against their persecutors, invisibly patrolling the ghetto by night, and preventing Christians from depositing dead children there to serve as false evidence of ritual murders.

The Evil Eye

In many parts of Europe there exists a belief related to witchcraft, but not identical with it—the notion of the Evil Eye, also called 'fascination', and *la jettatura*. The difference is that whereas witchcraft and sorcery are thought to be skills deliberately acquired and consciously used, the Eye is envisaged as a natural faculty. It may be innate (some add, hereditary), or may develop in infancy as a result of some error in child-rearing; in Greece, for instance, it is said that if a mother lets her baby resume suckling after she had started to wean it, it will grow up with the Evil Eye. Those who have it are sometimes said to be unable to control it, or even unaware that they have it; more often, however, it is associated with a malicious temperament. St Basil, in the fourth century, described its effects:

. . . some think that envious persons bring bad luck merely by a glance, so that healthy persons in the full flower and vigour of their prime are made to pine away under their spell, suddenly losing all their plumpness, which dwindles and wastes away under the gaze of the envious.

Quoted in Alan Dundes, 'Wet and Dry: The Evil Eye', in *Folklore Studies in the Twentieth Century*, ed. Venetia Newall, London and Totowa, 1980, p. 38.

irrational, is more acceptable than the disturbing thought that one's life is at the mercy of arbitrary chance. Moreover, the victim is not powerless but can take steps to avoid future trouble, since wherever the belief in the Evil Eye is found there are also traditional countermeasures, cures, and protective charms.

The range of these devices is enormous, from prayers and religious formulae in Gaelic-speaking Scotland, or the use of holy water and medals in Catholic countries, to ancient amulets rooted in pre-Christian cults. Of the latter, one is the representation of a benevolent eye, counteracting the Evil Eye on the well-known magical principle that 'like affects like'. It can be seen realistically painted on the prows of Mediterranean fishing boats, or rendered as a formal blue and white pattern on a blue glass bead, which is a favourite amulet in Greece and Turkey. This design has precedents in Classical Greece and Rome, and above all in ancient Egypt. Equally old is the representation of a phallus, commonly displayed throughout the Roman Empire to bring luck and fertility, and banish evil magical forces. Christianity disapproved of such overt sexuality, but amulets which are obviously modifications of the phallus are still very popular in Italy; they are pendants shaped like a slightly twisted horn, made from coral, amber, or polished metal—or, nowadays, from glossy red plastic. The glitter and redness are significant; they are meant to catch the attention of the person with the Evil Eye, since it is thought that his power is concentrated in his first glance, and that this will be neutralized if it falls on something as powerful as itself. Actual animal horns are also sometimes used, combining aggressive and sexual symbolism; thus, skulls of horned cattle (or plaster copies) are often displayed on walls and roofs of Maltese farms.

Verbal formulae, often sexually or anally obscene, are also held to be protective; so is spitting, and obscene gestures such as the *mano cornuta* (index finger and little finger extended as horns, with other fingers clenched), and the *mano fica* (thumb thrust between clenched fingers). More drastic sexual actions, such as baring one's

It also can injure animals, particularly farm livestock, blight crops and fruit trees, and destroy the luck of huntsmen and fishermen; in short, whatever person, possession or activity is both important and vulnerable to chance, is regarded as susceptible to the effects of the Evil Eye. Communities holding this belief are most reluctant to praise anyone or anything, or to mention a success or piece of luck, for fear of rousing envy, thus activating the malice of someone with the Eye, who would cause some calamity to befall them.

Like other theories about destructive supernatural forces, this is, paradoxically, psychologically helpful to people in misfortune. It allows them to blame their troubles onto someone else, and offers an explanation which, however genitals or buttocks, were probably once widespread in rural communities for magical purposes, but published references to such matters were understandably rare. Recent research in the Balkans has shown that ritual nudity was practised by Albanian, Serbian and Bosnian peasants as late as the 1940s to protect them from evil spells when they were engaged in dangerous work. If, for example, heavy timbers were being transported along difficult roads, a naked man would walk beside the cart, ostentatiously displaying his penis and joking about it, to divert the attention of evil-minded bystanders. To protect children from the Evil Eye, Albanian

Left. A twelfth-century carving formerly over the Porta Tosa, a gateway in Milan. The figure, with lifted skirt, is clipping her pubic hair with shears – a gesture possibly connected with the Italian folk belief that troublesome fairies will flee if challenged to straighten a pubic hair. Castello Sforzesco, Milan.

Below. A barn at Lattrop, in the Twente district of Holland. Its barge-boards are topped with stylized horse-heads, which brought good luck and protected the building from evil.

iron, holed stones, rowan twigs, and marigolds hung by the doors; various lucky trees and flowers in gardens; bones, shoes and bottles built into the foundations or walls. Every country had comparable charms; in Catholic areas there were, in addition, items with religious associations, such as the pebbles known as 'St Lucy's Eyes' in Sardinia and the amulet called 'St Paul's Tongue' in Malta, and of course medals of the Virgin and of various saints. It is common to see Catholic objects displayed side by side with amulets of pagan origin, for instance a rosary, a St Christopher medal and a phallic horn all hanging from a car's driving-mirror;

mothers would rub their own genitals and pat the child's face with the same hand; Balkan gypsy men would do the same to a horse's back if it could not draw its load. The life-giving force of sexuality, sometimes combined with that of laughter and/or with aggressive and contemptuous expressions, destroys the evil influence.

The amulets and gestures used

against the Evil Eye were also, for the most part, considered effective against witches too, and further protective devices were displayed on houses and farm buildings, especially near chimneys, windows and doors–the places where witches could gain entry. In Britain, they included carved oak posts beside the hearth; patterns chalked on the threshold; horseshoes, lumps of

the items are functionally equivalent, despite their diverse origins, and the users apparently find no incongruity between them.

Counter-spells
When, despite all precautions, misfortune strikes and witchcraft or the Evil Eye is suspected, counter-measures must be taken. In communities where

Above. Iron cocks, common on roofs of old houses in Moravia and Slovakia, were said to drive away demons, ghosts and witches. The cock symbolized the victory of light over darkness, and iron is a widespread charm against supernatural evil. Moravské Muzeum, Brno.

Above right. A 'witch-post' in a Yorkshire farm, said to stop witches coming down the chimney or laying a spell on the hearth. They are carved with patterns based on the St Andrew's Cross above several horizontal bands. Ryedale Folk Museum.

Right. Bellarmine jugs have been found in the floors or walls of several old houses in England, with contents such as threads, nails, pins, and animals hearts or cloth hearts, indicating that they had been used as 'witch-bottles'. The fierce face on these jugs may have made them popular for this purpose. Museum of London.

traditions were strong, victims often knew for themselves what must be done: if butter will not 'come', plunge a red-hot poker into the churn; if a cart sticks inexplicably in mud, flog its wheels or scrape them with a knife; if cattle are dying of contagious disease, cut the heart from a dead one, stick pins in it, and roast it slowly. For human sickness, fill a bottle with the victim's urine, add pins and knotted threads, and boil this 'witch-bottle' slowly by laying it near the hearth. All these were aggressive devices; the witch, it was thought, would feel the burning, flogging, pricking or cutting in her own body, and would be forced to lift her spell to escape the pain. If the victim does not know these rituals, or if they

fail, he can consult what in English was variously called a 'white witch', 'wise woman', 'cunning man', 'conjurer', or 'wizard'—a type of person formerly to be found in rural communities throughout Europe, whose role corresponded roughly to that of an African 'witch doctor'. This is a man or woman reputed to have paranormal abilities in diagnosing whether illnesses are caused by supernatural forces (whether witches, fairies, or demons), identifying the culprit, and performing magical remedies. As Keith Thomas has pointed out, the process involved some semi-conscious collusion between the victim and the 'conjurer', with the latter confirming the former's pre-existing assumptions:

The client would go to the local wizard, describe his symptoms, and invite diagnosis. After having recourse to one of a variety of magical aids, the wizard would be expected to pronounce as to whether or not the victim was indeed bewitched, and indicate the identity of the evil-doer. . . . The wizard's diagnosis of maleficium [bewitchment] *would not have been acceptable unless the patient himself found it plausible; and when it came to identifying the witch . . . all the wizard did was to confirm the suspicions already present in the client's mind. . . . The wizard would show the client a mirror or a piece of polished stone and ask if he recognised the face he saw in it. Or*

witch's face, cut off a lock of her hair, or stab her shadow or her footprint, in order to break her power.

Some 'wise women' and 'conjurers' preferred blessings and rituals based on Christian symbolism rather than aggressive counter-spells, and numerous examples of these have been recorded from the Middle Ages to the present day. Two must suffice here. One, known to have been used in London in 1622, is interesting for its allusion to the triple source of harmful magic, namely a malevolent heart, spoken spells or curses, and the glance of the Evil Eye: 'Three biters have bit him, heart, tongue, eye; three better shall help him, Father, Son, and Holy Ghost.' The other was the ritual employed by a 'wise

whether an illness sprang from natural causes, in which case she prescribed ordinary herbal cures, or from a spell to be broken by a ritual act. She had inherited her knowledge and power from her father, a man as devout as herself.

Amulets, counter-spells and prayers belong to the real world; the objects, actions and words involved are physical realities, however much the effects ascribed to them may be supernatural. The behaviour of the 'wise women' and 'conjurers' seems, from surviving accounts, to have been equally down-to-earth; they did not, for instance, fall into trances, see visions, or exhibit symptoms of spirit possession. Occasionally, however, one does find evidence of

he might ask the client for a list of suspects, and carry out a series of tests designed to isolate the guilty one, carefully watching for his customer's reaction as each name was pronounced.
Keith Thomas, *Religion and the Decline of Magic*, London and New York, 1971, p. 549.

Once the witch had been identified, counterspells of the type described above might be recommended, or the patient might be advised to scratch the

woman' on North Uist in the Hebrides in 1909, when a horse collapsed shortly after being praised by a man rumoured to have the Evil Eye. She took three threads to represent the Trinity (black for the Father, red for the Son, white for the Spirit), twined them into a cord, and showed the horse's owner how to tie it round the root of its tail in the name of the Trinity; the horse recovered at once. This woman's outlook was fervently Christian; not only did she rely on Trinitarian symbolism, but she believed that God revealed to her in prayer

communities where the struggle to eliminate the effects of witchcraft had itself become 'mythologized', i.e. transposed wholly into the realm of fantasy. In late sixteenth-century Italy, at Friuli, there existed a group of witch-fighters calling themselves *benandanti*, 'Doers of Good', whose activities have been studied by Carlo Ginzburg. They were peasant men who had been born with cauls (always an indication of good luck and preternatural powers, according to popular beliefs), and who had been further set apart by having been

Left. Illustration by Gustave Doré for Rabelais' mocking account of the consultation of a village 'wise woman' nicknamed the Sybil of Panzoust.

Left. A modern Scottish 'Luckenbooth' brooch, a type formerly worn by babies and pregnant women to guard them against witchcraft and the evil eye. The crowned heart is now said to allude to Mary Queen of Scots, but may well derive from Roman Catholic symbolism of the Sacred Heart of Jesus or of Mary; cf. Chapter Six, p. 86.

Below. An Austrian *Freisenkette*, to protect babies from convulsions (*Freise*) and from other evils. Assorted charms are strung on red cord; those here include a heart, hands making apotropaic gestures, holy medals, coins, hairs from a goat's beard, and a small triangular cloth bag called a *Breverl* containing written prayers and pictures of saints. Österreichisches Museum für Volkskunde, Vienna.

summoned by an angel in a dream to enrol in the *benandanti*. It was their task to go forth in the spirit, during the Ember days, to fight witches who were trying to destroy crops and murder children. Their souls rode to battle on goats, cats or horses, armed with stalks of fennel, while the witches wielded bunches of sorghum. Their bodies, meanwhile, lay in bed in a deep trance and could not be awakened throughout the three-day period. The outcome of this spiritual battle would determine the success or failure of the coming harvest. In their own eyes, the *benandanti* served Christ and their community, yet the Church condemned their beliefs, and the Inquisition accused them of holding diabolical sabbats, thus associating them with the very witches they were attacking. Here again, as in the cases of 'St Guinefort' and of the 'messenger of souls' at Montaillou (p. 85-6), Church authorities suppressed the unauthorized persons who were acting as intermediaries for their communities in dealing with supernatural beings, rather as British colonial administrators tried to suppress African witch-doctors. The *benandanti* were duly crushed, but elsewhere the village 'cunning men' and 'white witches' continued to serve the needs of their neighbours so long as any fear of witchcraft remained – which, in some cases, has lasted to the present time.

Mythology in Folk Festivals

The cycle of seasonal customs and annual festivities is complex, not only because every area develops individual variations, but because the timing of festivals is determined by several historically independent systems. Very few follow the astronomical calendar; true, midsummer is fairly accurately pinpointed by sports and bonfires held on 24 June in many countries, but the midwinter observances stretch across a range of dates in late December and early January. More influential is the annual cycle of food production, varying according to each region's main produce, and climate; arable farming sets a different pattern from animal husbandry, fruit-growing, fishing, the making of wine and beer. Each of these may generate festivals, marking the beginning of major activities (e.g. ploughing) or their conclusion (harvesting, vintaging, sheep-shearing). Transitions from periods of food scarcity to those of abundance are also frequent determinants – the many festivals of late autumn were made possible by the availability of ample wine, beer, corn, and freshly slaughtered meat at that season. Then there is the Church calendar, supplying not only the major cycle of Advent, Christmas, Lent, Easter, and Pentecost, but also saints' days and patronal festivals. Superimposed upon all these, come national celebrations, such as Independence Days, anniversaries of victories, etc.; these are not in themselves folkloric, being established by State authority, but alongside the official ceremonials there generally are relatively informal popular activities such as bonfires and dancing. Finally, some countries have added arbitrary Bank Holidays, which soon sprout local customs of their own (e.g. pageants, fairs, sports meetings).

Festivals are as diverse in content as in timing, often having both communal and individual aspects, and reflecting political and/or commercial influences alongside the 'purely' traditional – if, indeed, such purity ever exists! Strictly speaking, no festival should be regarded as a single custom, but as a network of interrelated activities, often fulfilling diverse purposes; thus, a holy day may be marked not only by church-going but by tolerated rowdyism and drunkenness, or a ritual dance is both a luck-bringing ceremony, a display of prestigious skill, and a means of earning money. It is beyond the scope of this book to explore all these facets; it is enough to pick out a few aspects which can be shown to relate to the 'mythological' side of European folklore.

Survivals of Pre-Christian Festivals?

Explicit traces of pre-Christian deities are extremely rare, despite the readiness of Puritan preachers to identify Christmas with the Roman Saturnalia, and Maypoles with idols of Baal. The denunciations of medieval clerics, who called it 'devilish' to take part in certain dances or to disguise oneself as an animal, have seemed to many scholars evidence of survival of pagan cults, but are by no means conclusive; priests might easily have thought a custom damnable and devil-inspired simply because it expressed sexuality, or encouraged drunkenness, or led to lawlessness, or because it included men dressing as women, contrary to Biblical injunctions. All this might make it 'devilish' in their eyes, without any element of honouring a 'devil', i.e. a pagan supernatural being. Even those nineteenth-century folklorists who were most firmly convinced that many

customs originated in sun-worship or fertility cults relied mainly upon analogies with similar customs in non-Christian societies to interpret the Christian European material.

When festivals honouring ancient gods do survive, they are so modified as to be barely recognizable. On 1 August in pagan Ireland there was a festival named Lughnasad, the 'Assembly' or 'Games' of Lugh–Lugh being a vigorous young god of many skills, worshipped in Ireland and Gaul. In modern Irish, 1 August is still called Lughnasad, and is traditionally the day for digging up the first potatoes of the new crop, thus inaugurating a welcome period of plentiful food, but no ceremony marks the date. Until recently, however, there was a festival either on the last Sunday in July or the first in August, variously known as 'First Sunday in Harvest', 'Mountain Sunday', 'Garland Sunday', or 'Bilberry Sunday': one text alone calls it 'Lugnasa Sunday'. It consisted of a cheerful gathering on a hill-top or at some other landmark, with dancing, wrestling, racing, picking bilberries and wild flowers, wooing, and sometimes brief fights. According to some stories, it commemorated St Patrick's conflict with a pagan ruler, whom he killed, or converted through a miracle, e.g. by killing and resuscitating a bull. After thorough analysis of all the traditions about this festival, Maíre Mac Neil concluded that it is a continuation of the pagan Lughnasa, with St Patrick replacing Lugh as hero; originally, she claims, it celebrated Lugh's annual victory over a divine rival whose possessions (corn and bull) he gave to the people as a very bountiful harvest. Though this

reconstruction may well be historically correct, it is obvious from the many written and oral descriptions of the modern festival which she quotes that all participants were entirely unaware of any mythological substratum to their merrymaking. A mythological element discernible only to the skilled eye of a scholar is of great theoretical interest, but cannot be considered part of the living significance which the event holds for those taking part. Memories of major pagan gods faded so completely that European customs, like European folktales, show only faint, distorted traces of their existence.

In contrast, minor supernatural beings – fairies, spirits, witches – are frequently connected with seasonal rituals, in a negative role. They are imagined as exerting increased malevolence at specified times of the year, and the customs carried out then are said to counteract their influence and replace it with renewed prosperity and luck. These times of critical danger often coincide either with high points in the Church calendar or with seasons of important agricultural activity. In British traditions, Halloween is a good example. It falls on the eve of a major Church feast, All Saints' Day, thus illustrating a widespread belief that menacing forces are let loose during the night preceding a sacred day – one may compare Continental beliefs about the witches' gatherings on Midsummer Eve and on Walpurgis Night (30 April, eve of May Day). Going further back in time, one finds that Celtic societies reckoned 1 November as their New Year's Day, bringing their cattle back into winter quarters on this date. Medieval Irish texts make clear that all manner of evil beings, ghosts and fairies were believed to be powerful at Halloween, and it is reasonable to assume that the customary bonfires, disguises and mischief-

making were originally intended to counteract their malevolence, even though this purpose later became obscured.

Benevolent fairies, too, have a role in certain festivals, especially Christmas and related winter feasts. Some are said to bring seasonal gifts, as described below. Others, notably the *nisse* and *tomte*, the guardian house-spirit of Scandinavian farms, must by tradition be given fine porridge or other dainty foods on Christmas Eve; if they were neglected, their anger would be aroused.

Căluș: The Exorcizing Dance

One ritual where the aim of defeating dangerous spirits is still explicit is the Căluș dance of southern Romania, performed on Whit Sunday and during Whit-week, a period there known as Rusalii. This season in some ways resembles a 'new year': winter gives way to warmer weather, work starts in the fields, the earliest fruits appear, spring cleaning is done. Magically, however, it is a perilous time: the dead visit their former homes on Whit Sunday, and both devils and the malevolent *iele* (the fairies described in Chapter Four, p. 49-50) are particularly threatening throughout Rusalii. All week, people observe taboos against various activities which would be appropriate to the season: nobody must do farm work, climb fruit trees, clean the house, or even wash oneself, on pain of being 'possessed' by the *iele*, which would induce giddiness, tremors, and hysterical bewilderment. Besides observing the taboos, people try to protect themselves by wearing garlic and wormwood, but their chief defence—and the only cure for anybody who becomes possessed—is the ritual dance known as Căluș.

It is performed by a group of seven, nine or eleven men called Călușari, who form a brotherhood bound by oaths of obedience to their leader. This leader knows secret healing charms, and preserves the accuracy of the rituals. Another important individual within the group is the 'mute', a masked clown-like figure whose bawdy and disruptive antics alternate with the serious, intricate group dancing; his costume is grotesque, and always includes some female garment, usually a skirt or

Breughel, *The Fight between Carnival and Lent*, 1559. Details in this scene include two folk-plays being performed outside inns, on the left side of the painting. In the middle distance, a man in shaggy clothes and a tangled wig impersonates 'The Foul Bride'; in the far distance, a group enacts the capture of a Wild Man by an archer, a woman, and an emperor. Kunsthistorisches Museum, Vienna.

village, dancing in the courtyard of every house in turn. Wherever they dance there will be good luck and good health, for their arrival expels dangerous spirits; conversely, anyone who refused to welcome them would incur calamity. The performance consists of a suite of complicated, spectacular dances, periodically interrupted by farcical interludes; for instance, the mute may chase women and children and tap them with a wooden phallus, or he and some of the dancers may improvise brief playlets full of slapstick humour and bawdy jokes. The dancing and the foolery are both considered sources of vitality, health and good luck for the community. It is believed that the women touched by the phallus will bear children soon, and that those who can pull garlic from a dancer's belt, or a thread from his clothing, will keep their husbands faithful. Salt, wheat, garlic, wool, and a bowl of water are customarily placed in the centre of the space where the Călușari dance, so that there should be good crops, good rain, and health for the livestock; after the performance, people rush to get the garlic for use as a cure throughout the year. Having been paid for their services, the Călușari move on to the next house.

apron. The rest of the Călușari wear embroidered white shirts, with woven cross-bands and decorated hats; they sometimes wear bells on their legs, or jingling spurs, to drive away evil spirits with noise, and constantly chew garlic and wormwood, the smell of which is held to repel the spirits. They carry wooden sticks, and are accompanied by musicians and a flag-bearer. According to eighteenth-century accounts, their costume was formerly a transvestite disguise; at that time, the whole troupe wore women's dress, with white veils hiding their faces, and spoke in falsetto, though they also carried swords, therefore preserving one element of masculinity.

The ritual begins on Whit-Saturday, when the Călușari gather privately at a crossroads or other remote spot to take their oath and raise their flag, thus inaugurating the sacred period. On the Sunday morning they begin touring the

Opposite top. Ducking for apples at Halloween, c. 1860. This feast was formerly a time for divinations and for house-to-house visiting by masked guisers, especially in Scotland. It is now mainly a children's festival, to which guising has returned in the American form known as 'trick or treat'.

Opposite bottom. A group of Călușari at a Rumanian fair, 1928. One is riding a hobby-horse, which is probably an original feature of the custom, though rare in the twentieth century; *căluș* means 'little horse'.

Right. An Austrian mummer impersonating a 'Wild Man'. From the Middle Ages on, the Wild Man – a hairy, savage, half-human creature – has figured in literature, art, pageantry, and folk-custom as a threatening monster to be tamed or defeated.

Below 'Fair Perchtas', Salzburg, Austria. Wearing national costume and carrying decorated banners and garlands, these represent the benevolent aspect of midwinter spirits, in contrast to the band of 'Frightful Perchtas' shown in Chapter Four, p. 48.

Above. Guy Fawkes, by F. D. Bedford, about 1905. Once a serious political commemoration, 5 November has become a children's festival. Deep-rooted behaviour-patterns reappear: masking, parading, demanding money from householders and passers-by, burning effigies, making a cheerful uproar. The result is a mini-carnival in winter.

Right. The Abbots Bromley Horn Dance, Staffordshire. In this ritual, first described in 1686, six morris dancers carry antlers; there is also a 'woman' an archer, a fool, and sometimes a hobby-horse. It is a dance only, not a play, but the antler-bearers do menace each other.

If it happens that someone, having broken the Rusalii taboos, falls ill with symptoms indicating possession, the Călușari must diagnose and heal her (it is generally a woman) by a dramatic ritual of exorcism. This is not a public rite; it takes place at a crossroads or some other spot on the outskirts of the village, and any onlookers must remain at a good distance. The patient lies on the ground, and the Călușari dance round her and jump over her, until the leader of the group induces one of them to fall down in a trance; he then smashes a pot and kills a chicken, whereupon the woman rises unsteadily to her feet, supported by two Călușari. The unconscious dancer, who is held to have 'given his health' to the patient, is recalled from his trance, and the procedure is then repeated twice more to complete the healing. In return, the patient undertakes to feed the whole Călușari team during the Rusalii days for three years, and/or to dance a special dance

with them at their healing sessions.

The relation of the Călușari to the fairies, the *iele*, has been much debated. Several Romanian scholars hold that they represent or personify the *iele*, by wearing white and dancing in a ring so fast that their feet seem to 'fly'; the old descriptions of their female costume strongly supports this argument. Some of the dancers themselves, especially the older ones, maintain that 'Căluș comes

from the *iele*'–i.e. that fairies originally taught the dances to the first Călușari. This exemplifies a common tendency, noted in Chapter Four (pp. 56, 64-5), to ascribe the skills of outstanding musicians or healers to fairy teachers or fairy ancestors. On the other hand, as Gail Kligman points out in her masterly study of this ritual (*Căluș*, 1981), the dancers are equally emphatic that their performance is done 'so that the *iele* don't come to harm people'; they see themselves as defending their village from supernatural attack. Either way, mythological significance is central to the custom; the clarity with which it is expressed in this Romanian tradition helps one to recognize similar traits in disguised and eroded forms elsewhere.

Midwinter Giftbringers and Bogies

Supernatural beings are very prominent in midwinter customs throughout Europe, coming by night as gift-bringers or as mock-malevolent bogies;

food and water with their urine if not kept at bay by hanging up bunches of hyssop and asparagus, or burning bits of old leather. In Scandinavia, it was necessary to prepare a welcome for the elves who, it was said, invaded human homes on Christmas Eve and New Year's Eve to feast and dance there while everyone was at church; the house must be thoroughly cleaned, lights left burning and all doors open, and sometimes food was set out for them. In Iceland the housewife would repeat a formula of cautious welcome before leaving: 'Let them come who wish to come, and let them go who wish to go, and do no harm to me or mine.'

Normally, however, the legendary Christmas visitants are taken quite light-heartedly. In Germany it is Holda or Perchta who comes to reward good children and punish naughty ones; in some areas she is impersonated by an adult who surreptitiously tosses sweets and presents into children's rooms. More dramatic are the masked 'Berchten' or 'Perchten' of Bavaria and Austria, bands of whom roam the streets, armed with brooms, pitchforks and chains, going from house to house to demand money in exchange for the good luck their visit brings. Italy has a kindly witch called La Befana ('Epiphany'), bringing gifts on Twelfth Night; she is said to be a woman who got to Bethlehem too late to worship the Baby Jesus, and was condemned to wander forever and give gifts to every child. In parts of Tuscany groups of guisers impersonate her, her husband Befano, and their attendants; all are dressed in scruffy old clothes, with blackened faces and 'hair' made from old rope, while Befana and Befano are padded to look hunchbacked. They are accompanied by musicians, and a live horse or donkey. At each house they dance, sing about the (imaginary) presents they are bringing, and wish the family luck; in return they get a glass of wine, a little food, or a little money. The children later find sweets, oranges and toys in their stockings, supposedly brought by La Befana but of course supplied by their parents.

The most famous gift-bringer is St Nicholas/Santa Claus/Father Christmas, whether he be dressed as a Bishop or as an old man in a red gown, and whether he operates on 6 December, his ecclesiastical feastday, or on Christmas Eve. Originally, he punished naughty children as well as rewarding good ones; in parts of Germany he carries a stick and a 'black book' recording their misdeeds, while in many countries he is accompanied by a comic black-faced hobgoblin variously known as Black Peter, Krampus, Ruprecht, Hans Scruff, etc., who whips those who deserve it. Both the Saint and his attendant are frequently impersonated, either by adults at home to impress the children, or in a communal ceremony, as in Amsterdam, where an official St Nicholas sails into the harbour, supposedly from Spain. Occasionally his visitation is turned into a more generalized luck-bringing and apotropaic custom to benefit the whole household; at Berchtesgarden on the first Sunday in Advent, St Nicholas, two Krampuses, and twelve masked men with bells and chains run from house to house, reciting prayers and making as much noise as possible, to drive out evil spirits.

Christmas visitants may develop into threatening bogies, for scaring children into good behaviour. In Icelandic tradition there is a fine specimen—a hideous she-troll called Grýla, with fifteen tails, a hundred bags tied to each tail, and twenty naughty children captive in each bag. She has thirteen terrifying sons, who appear, one by one, in the thirteen days preceding Christmas Day, and depart similarly one by one between Christmas and Twelfth Night. All were supposedly eager to pounce on naughty children and gobble them up. There have been mock-horror rhymes describing Grýla and her sons from the sixteenth to the mid-twentieth centuries, but nowadays, with gentler methods of upbringing, children are more likely to be told that Grýla's sons will pop presents under their pillows.

As the year begins, one encounters many customs designed to mark the start of cultivation, e.g. first ploughing, or looking ahead to future crops, e.g. wassailing apples. They incorporate some actions which, in general terms, symbolize and thus ensure good luck and prosperity, and others whose aggressiveness implies the driving off of

sometimes they are merely spoken of, but often they are impersonated by men and women in disguise. The problem with midwinter supernatural visitants, from the folklorist's point of view, is that though there is abundant material about them it is impossible to assess how seriously it was taken in earlier generations; nowadays they are simply figures of fantasy with which adults entertain (or frighten) children, but the situation may have been different 200 years ago. In some regions, an aura of fear does seem to cling to these beings, even in fairly recent times; thus, the Greeks held that grotesque, deformed goblins called Kallicantzaroi lurked round their farms during the twelve days of Christmas, and would pollute

Left. Carnival Masquerader at Skyros, Greece, 1906, wearing a sheepskin mask and hood and sheep bells. He was accompanied by his 'wife', a boy dressed as a girl. In Thrace similar mummers threw grain in the streets, offered wine to householders, and were ducked in rivers.

Right. Carnival Bear at Pratz de Mollo, French Pyrenees. On 2 February a 'bear' runs wild through the town, smearing people with sooty paws, till he is caught and led in chains by a 'barber' dressed as a woman, who pretends to shave him and dances with him.

evil forces – e.g. firing guns, shouting, stamping, blowing horns, lighting fires. Some scholars have regarded bonfires primarily as relics of sun worship, aimed at encouraging the sun's return when held at midwinter, and at celebrating it when held at midsummer. As a theory of origins this is quite plausible, but in actual living beliefs the apotropaic function of fire was, and is, more prominent. In Germany, incense is traditionally burned in homes and stables on 'the Twelve Smoke Nights' (25 December to 6 January), to drive away the spectral Wild Hunt. In nineteenth-century Herefordshire farmers lit thirteen bonfires on each wheatfield on 5 January to 'burn the witches', drinking cider and shouting and cheer-

ing; otherwise, they said, there would be no good crop. Midsummer bonfires were equally protective, especially against witches; in many countries, cattle were driven through the smoke to strengthen them against diseases caused by witchcraft.

Ritual Disguise

One vexed question in folklore is the interpretation of 'guising' or 'mumming', which constantly crops up in various forms in European seasonal customs. The essence of it is that the performer(s) of some ritualized action (which may be as simple as house-to-house visiting, or an elaborate dance or drama) conceals his identity behind some disguise, the choice of which is

dictated by tradition, not left to his personal fancy. The disguises vary locally – leaves, flowers, animal skins, masks, veils, straw, paper streamers, blackened faces, women's clothing, or any combination of these – but are always cheap and readily available, unlike the elaborate and individualistic fancy dress of a Carnival. The underlying symbolism has been hotly debated. Some scholars think their purpose is to scare away ghosts, demons, fairies or witches by their ugliness, or break their spells by causing laughter and, in some cases, by sexual display. Others stress the anonymity they give the performers, which, like priestly robes, sets them apart from the everyday world and puts them in contact with the supernatural.

Certain disguises, it is argued, actually identify a performer with a supernatural being; by dressing in greenery, for instance, he incarnates the spirit of spring vegetation. The debate has had to rely mainly upon theory and upon anthropological parallels from distant cultures, since the statements made by performers as to their beliefs and intentions are too scanty, and too

Above. La Tarasque, the she-dragon of Tarascon, France. The men in knee-breeches are two of the Tarascaires, a team of dancers who escort her with drums, sing nonsense verses, and dance the Farandole. To touch the Tarasque brings good luck.

Right. Midsummer Bonfires in Brittany, 1893. The occasion is partly religious in intention, being held on the eve of St John's Day; in the background is a large *Calvaire*, an open-air crucifix. It also expresses local patriotism, for the dancers are wearing their regional costume.

inconsistent, to form a basis for a general solution. It is in any case probable that guising has always fulfilled several functions simultaneously, only some of them being directed towards 'supernatural' or magical ends, while the rest concern the effect produced by the disguise on the audience (fear, amusement, admiration, puzzlement) or on the wearer himself

Le Petit Journal

TOUS LES JOURS
Le Petit Journal
5 Centimes

SUPPLÉMENT ILLUSTRÉ
Huit pages : CINQ centimes

TOUS LES VENDREDIS
Le Supplément illustré
5 Centimes

Quatrième Année   SAMEDI 1ᵉʳ JUILLET 1893   Numéro 136

Les feux de la Saint-Jean en Bretagne

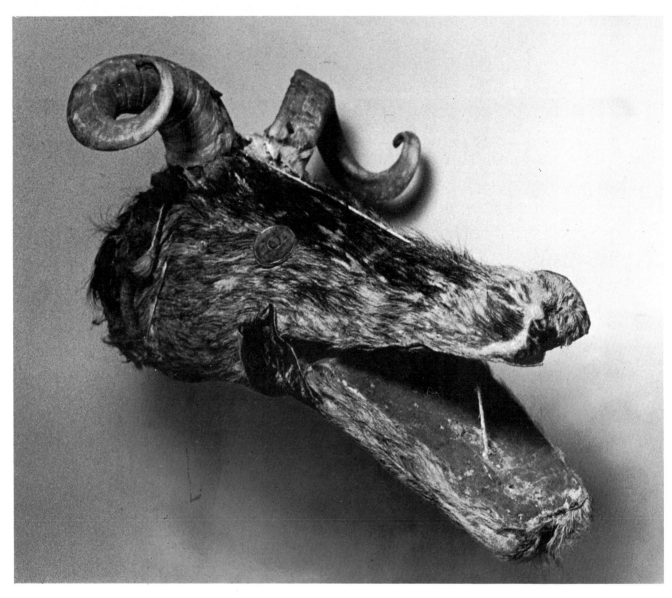

(release from conventional restraints, enjoyment of power, mild psychological dissociation).

One intriguing form of disguise consists of a man impersonating an animal, generally by wearing or carrying its head while concealing himself in draperies. All the British examples are analyzed by E. C. Cawte in his *Ritual Animal Disguise* (1978). They include the Mari Lwyd in Wales and the Wild Horse at Antrobus in Cheshire, both consisting of a horse skull with articulated jaws, mounted on a short pole and carried by a stooping man hidden under a cloth; the Kentish Hooden Horses, on taller poles and with wooden heads; the Derbyshire Old Tup (i.e. ram), made from a real or an imitation sheep's head and a sheepskin or sack. The Mari Lwyd and Hooden Horses were led from house to house around Christmas; the Antrobus Wild Horse still provides the main farcical element in a Mummers' Play in early November; Old Tup was the hero of a Christmas or New Year's play, in which he was stabbed by a Butcher and revived by a Doctor. All these performances involved rough humour and mock aggression; the animal chased people, snapped at them, kicked its accompanying groom or jockey, and so on. Old Tup is particularly interesting for his death and resurrection, a common theme in seasonal folk rituals.

Similar animal disguises occur in many parts of Europe, and there are disapproving references to them by several early Christian writers. St Augustine warns in a sermon: 'If you ever hear of anyone carrying on that most filthy practice of dressing up as a horse or a stag, punish him most severely.' It seems that then, as now, they performed at mid-winter, going from house to house; Caesarius of Arles (470-542) condemns men who wear animals' heads or women's clothes on the calends (first day) of January, and urges his hearers: 'Do not allow a stag or a calf or any monster to come in front of your house.' Modern customs from Eastern and Central Europe, particularly Poland, Czechoslovakia and parts of Germany and Austria, were described by Georges Dumézil (*Le Problème des Centaures*, 1929). There, guisers dressed as horses, goats or bears visit houses and ask for food and drink; they behave rowdily, and delight in chasing girls. In Scandinavia there is the Julbok ('Christmas goat'), which for-

merly appeared at weddings with a 'female' companion who, as in most traditional rituals, was a man in skirts. In the French Pyrenees, bears, horses and bulls come out at Shrovetide, giving performances with explicitly sexual elements; these customs, described by Violet Alford in 1928 and 1930, included a marriage between a bear and a 'woman' at Arles-sur-Tech, and elaborate parades of dancers at La Soule, in the course of which a horse was 'gelded' (two corks being tossed to the crowd), but recovered in a series of triumphant leaps. Throughout Europe, certain patterns recur: the animal is accompanied by a 'woman' and various grotesque companions, and sometimes by serious singers and dancers; its attendants struggle ludicrously to shoe it, ride it, or shave it, usually in vain;

there are coarse jokes; it dies, and revives. Most scholars believe that behind this foolery and the vague talk of the good luck it brings there was once a more specific intention of promoting agricultural fertility by mimicking the irrepressible sexuality of powerful male animals. It is a persuasive interpretation, though there is no way of proving it.

Dragon Parades

Certain other animal effigies, however, represent evil forces to be defeated. On Trinity Sunday at Mons in Belgium, a dragon, manoeuvered by several men, parades with an escort of devils, leaf-clad 'wild men', hobby-horses, clowns, and so on. It attacks onlookers with its tail, while they try to pluck off its hairs and ribbons for luck; eventually it is

killed in the main square by someone impersonating either St Georges or a local hero, Gilles de Chin. There used to be a similar pageant at Metz (France), in honour of St Clement, its first Bishop, who is said to have killed a dragon called Graoully, an effigy of which is still kept in the cathedral. These parades probably derive from a Catholic custom, best attested in pre-Revolutionary France, of including a dragon effigy in the religious processions round parish boundaries on Rogation Days, and battering it to pieces at the end, because it represented the Devil. They were all large-scale celebrations, requiring full communal involvement, elaborate costumes, and solidly-built, expensive effigies; they stand in contrast to the simpler, more home-made outfits of traditional winter guizers.

Possibly the most interesting of the dragon parades is the one at Tarasçon, in southern France. The dragon is a female, La Tarasque, represented by a wooden effigy so heavy that it was formerly manipulated by six men hidden in its hollow body, and nowadays is drawn on a wheeled frame; the present effigy, made in 1840, is the latest in a series going back to 1465. Before the Revolution, La Tarasque always came out twice a year, on Whit Monday and on St Martha's Day (29 July): later, its appearances grew rare, but there have been modern revivals. The two traditional events are markedly contrasted. On 29 July there was a religious procession, the docile monster being led to church by a little girl representing St Martha, who sprinkled holy water on it whenever its bearers briefly made it

erupted from its nostrils, its jaws snapped, and it knocked people over with wild sweeps of its wooden tail, to the delight of the crowds. Eventually it bowed three times outside St Martha's Church, and went home; the rest of the day was spent in boisterous sports and drinking.

There are several references to English dragon effigies in parish records in the fifteenth and sixteenth centuries, used in processions or plays in honour of St George or St Margaret – both reputedly dragon-slayers. One which survived the Reformation was Snap of Norwich, who evolved from a religious dragon belonging to the fourteenth-century Guild of St George into a civic dragon, appearing in the Mayor's inaugural procession at Midsummer until 1835; the figure then in use, made

guizers' beasts, and are not as old, they have acquired a popularity which goes far beyond their ecclesiastical role as symbols of Satan. Their grotesque appearance and vigorous, aggressive actions create a carnival atmosphere, in which mischief becomes temporarily acceptable.

Fire-walking

In Catholic countries, where holy days are celebrated with merrymaking as well as churchgoing, religious rites and secular customs often blend into a complex festival which the participants experience as an integrated whole, though observers from outside the community may respond with amazement, or even disapproval, at some bizarre elements. Perhaps the most dramatic of these is the ancient,

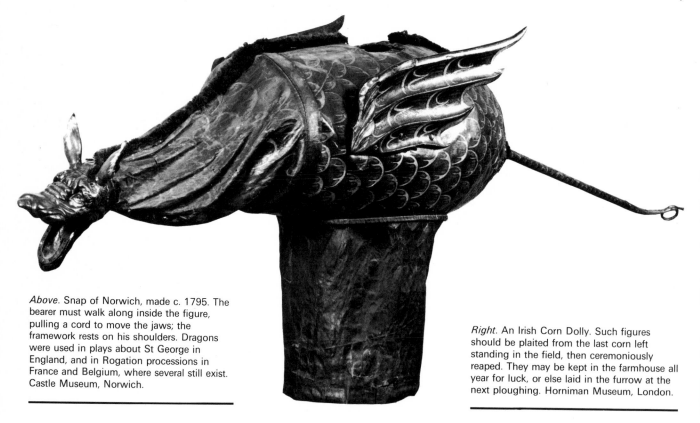

Above. Snap of Norwich, made c. 1795. The bearer must walk along inside the figure, pulling a cord to move the jaws; the framework rests on his shoulders. Dragons were used in plays about St George in England, and in Rogation processions in France and Belgium, where several still exist. Castle Museum, Norwich.

Right. An Irish Corn Dolly. Such figures should be plaited from the last corn left standing in the field, then ceremoniously reaped. They may be kept in the farmhouse all year for luck, or else laid in the furrow at the next ploughing. Horniman Museum, London.

swerve and snap its jaws. This illustrates a twelfth-century legend about how St Martha saved Tarasçon from a man-eating dragon in the Rhone, subduing it with holy water and leading it captive with her girdle for the townsfolk to kill. But on Whit Monday, things were much livelier. La Tarasque rushed through the streets, accompanied by dancing men; fireworks

about 1795, is still preserved. Other effigies imitating Snap were used in and around Norwich on less formal occasions up to the early years of this century. They gave great amusement by their antics, such as chasing and snapping at people, and swallowing coins in their clacking jaws. Although dragon-figures do not reflect such archaic folk beliefs as the midwinter

mysterious art of walking barefoot over red hot embers (known in cultures as diverse as Japan, ancient Rome, India and Polynesia), which survives in Europe in the context of two Church festivals in Greece and Spain.

The Greek ceremonies are held in Langhadas, a village near Salonika, on 21 May, the feast of Saints Constantine and Helena, to honour icons of these

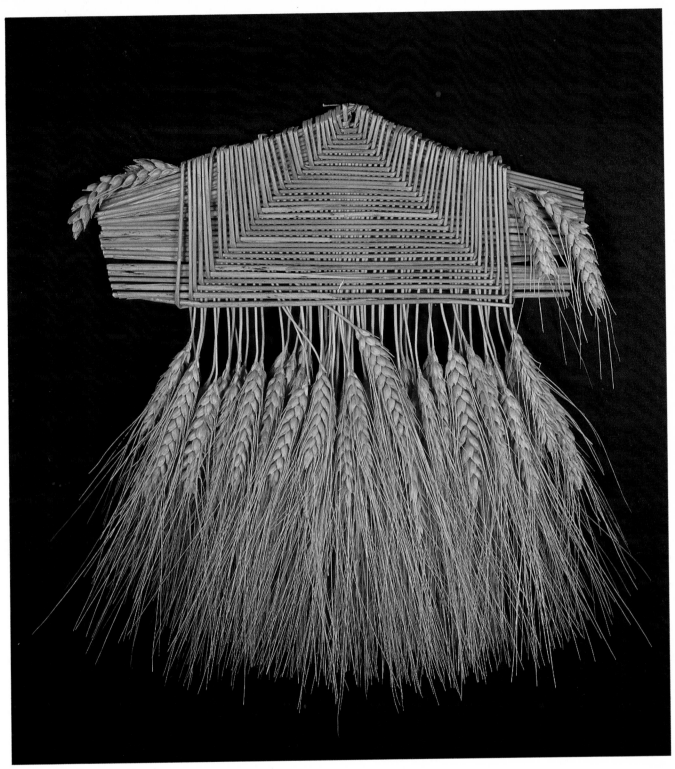

saints. The icons, and the custom, were brought to Langhadas in 1914 by refugees from Kostí in Thrace (now Bulgaria). In the thirteenth century, according to their legends, a church in Kostí had caught fire, but the icons inside it groaned so loudly that men ran into the flames to save them, and miraculously emerged unhurt; their descendants formed a religious guild called Anastenarides ('Groaners'), and still hold their annual festival to commemorate the event. On the morning of these saints' day, a young, uncastrated bull and ram are slaughtered, and roasted, to the accompaniment of loud, incessant drumming; their meat is for the Anastenarides, but their heads, hooves and skins are secretly buried. In the afternoon the icons are brought in procession from the church to an open space, where the embers of a large bonfire have been raked level and are still glowing intensely; the icon-bearers dance across the embers, to the heavy beat of the drums, emitting their characteristic groans, and singing a long ballad about 'Little Konstantinos'—a warrior whom they identify with St Constantine, although the ballad and

the Saint's life have nothing in common. The fire-dance lasts about twenty minutes, till the embers begin to cool, after which music and drinking continues in the taverns. The Greek Church condemns this festival as 'idolatrous', presumably because some scholars have tried to link it with the pagan cult of Dionysius; nevertheless, the Anastenarides themselves are devout Christians, convinced that the saints are present with them, preserving them from the fire.

In Spain, firewalking occurs at San Pedro Manrique on Midsummer Eve (a common date for bonfire rituals) as a preliminary to the feast of St John on 24 June. It is under the patronage of the Virgin Mary of their local church, La Peña, and the fire-walkers ascribe their success to their faith in her. A huge bonfire is lit about 6.00 p.m., and by midnight its embers have been raked out into a glowing carpet three or four

yards long and several inches thick, which barefooted men and girls cross one by one, with a rapid, firm tread, each carrying another person on his/her back. There is silence as they cross, but cheering and bursts of music after each has finished. No clergy are present, possibly as a sign of disapproval, but everyone else is there, led by the Mayor and Council and three elaborately costumed girls called Móndidas ('Pure Ones') chosen by lot from among young local virgins. Early next morning, St John's Day, the Móndidas take heavy baskets of ornamental loaves to church to be blessed, and then carry them round the town on their heads. Meanwhile, the Mayor and Council circumambulate the town walls and then preside at horse races in the square. At noon, the Móndidas bring the loaves back to the church, where everyone hears High Mass. In the afternoon, the Móndidas recite a long patriotic poem

Above. Christmas Mummers, 1861, by A. Hunt. Folk customs are not insulated from the socio-economic context of their times. In nineteenth-century England, farm labourers on low wages were glad of the money and beer the gentry gave them for their annual performances.

Above left. A drawing from R. M. Dawkins' account of carnival plays at Viza in Thrace, Greece, in 1906. The mummer with his face hidden in a stuffed goatskin hood has 'killed' another, similarly dressed; the latter's 'bride' mourns him, and two 'gypsies' watch.

Left. The slain mummer has revived, and the whole troupe goes round the village square pulling a plough and followed by a man scattering seed (not shown here).

about a defeat of the Moors in 844 A.D., and the rest of the day is spent in dancing.

Thus the fire-walking, however archaic its remote origins, is embedded into a religious and civic celebration whose other features are commonplace in Mediterranean festivals – the blessing of ornamental loaves, for instance, and the leading role given to young virgins. The 'mythology' of European fire-walking is now wholly Christian; it testifies to the power of faith, especially faith in a local sacred image (the icons at Langhadas, the statue of the Virgin of La Peña), and is dedicated to the honour of the saints. It would be a distortion of its living, complex characteristics to take the fire-walking in isolation and view it exclusively as a 'survival of paganism'.

Mummers' Plays and Harvest Customs

In their efforts to uncover pre-Christian rituals within European folklore, scholars have given particular attention to two categories of custom: mummers' plays and harvest ceremonies. Both have often been seen as survivals of fertility cults, with traces of human and animal sacrifices. These interpretations held the field almost unopposed from the time of Mannhardt and Frazer till after the Second World War, but are now increasingly criticized as speculations lacking enough evidence to carry conviction.

'Mummers' Plays' or 'Folk Drama' is a broad term for various traditional plays performed seasonally in streets or pubs or private houses by teams of men collecting money. They are short and farcical, using slapstick, comic patter, and grotesque costumes; their plots always involve death and resurrection, and sometimes also sex and birth. Full, uninhibited examples were to be found in the Balkans early in this century, for instance a Carnival performance in Thrace described by R. M. Dawkins. It included a marriage between a man concealed in an animal skin and a 'bride', and obscene foolery between a 'gypsy' and an 'old woman' in rags who carried a bundle representing a bastard baby. The 'bride' and 'old woman' were men in female garb, as usual in all guising. The 'bridegroom' was killed by a rival, lamented by his 'bride', and then suddenly revived. Finally the team paraded with a plough, scattering seeds and shouting 'May wheat be ten piastres the bushel!' Other plays of this type in Macedonia have the bridegroom resurrected by a comic doctor, a personage who regularly appears in many countries' versions.

In England, the great majority of surviving and recorded folk plays are of the type dubbed 'Hero-Combat Play'; they consist of a series of mock battles between pairs of boastful warriors, the hero being often 'King George' or 'St George', and his adversaries 'Bold Slasher', 'Black Prince', etc. Eventually one or more of the combatants falls dead, a comic doctor is summoned and revives him, a farcical character in grotesque disguise takes a collection, and the performance ends. The text of the play, which is fairly stable, contains nothing sexual, but occasional touches of bawdiness occur in performance; for instance, the doctor reviving the fallen fighter may let off a firework close to his genitals. Not too much weight should be attached to this; modern mumming teams know perfectly well that scholars have long regarded their play as a fertility rite, and this awareness, combined with the public's increased toleration of bawdy humour even in front of mixed audiences, may well feed back into their performances.

The other type of English ritual drama, the 'Wooing Play' of the East Midlands, is rarer, but closer to the presumed archaic prototype. A young 'female' is wooed by two or more men,

and chooses the Clown; occasionally the Clown is also pestered by an older 'female' who accuses him of fathering her bastard. There follows a fight in which someone – though not the Clown or the rival wooer(s) – is killed, and then revived by a doctor. The death-and-revival theme also occurs in the Sword Dances of North East England, involving the 'decapitation' of one dancer by the interlinked swords of the rest, and in the May Day dance of the Padstow Hobby-Horse, which repeatedly collapses and dies, but leaps up again when prodded by its attendant's club.

Harvest ceremonies were central to Frazer's famous theory that the ancient theme of a slain and resurrected vegetation god survives in folklore. The evidence, comprising descriptions from many parts of Europe, is consistent in its main features. A spirit lurks in the cornfield to guard it, in the shape of a fearsome hag or animal (see p. 53). The process of reaping and/or threshing was called 'killing' this creature; the last sheaf, or the slowest reaper, or both, was identified with it and became the focus for celebratory and luck-bringing rituals. Common among these were cutting the sheaf by flinging sickles at it from a distance; garlanding it, or the man who cut it; twisting its stalks into human or animal form; carrying this in procession; chasing, mocking or drenching its bearer; keeping and displaying it for a year for luck. All such ceremonies, argued Frazer and his predecessor Mannhardt, were softened versions of ancient sacrifices in which an animal or a man, incarnating the Corn Spirit, was killed to bring fertility to the crops. So too were customs where reapers or threshers would seize their employer, or a casual passer-by, and tie him up with straw ropes till he promised to pay for their drinks, give them cakes, provide a harvest supper, or tip them.

As ever, Frazer has to turn to very remote cultures to find unambiguous examples to clinch his argument; in this case, to Amerindians in Ecuador, Bechuana in Benin, Gonds and Khonds in India, all of whom are known to have formerly made human sacrifices for good harvests. His only European evidence comes from an ancient Greek legend about a Phrygian named Lity-

The Harvest Home, by Thomas Rowlandson, 1821. Whatever their origins, folk customs would soon die out if people did not enjoy them.

erses, who used to challenge passing strangers to a competition in reaping, make them drunk, and then wrap them up in corn, cut their heads off with a sickle, and throw the corpses in a river; eventually Herakles served him as he had served others. This is the only substantial analogy from Europe which Frazer can adduce; whether it is strong enough to bear the weight laid upon it must remain doubtful.

To a functionalist folklorist, the argument by archaic analogies is in any case irrelevant. I have already quoted (p. 15) von Sydow's retort that the Corn Spirit is nothing more than a bogy-figure used for scaring children away from crops, and it is easy to see equally practical reasons for other aspects of the complex of harvest customs. For instance, the tips extracted from employers or passers-by by pretended threats would be a welcome supplement to wages, and the accompanying rough play no doubt pleasurable; similar jocular 'demanding with menaces' occurs in other folk customs, e.g. when barring the route of wedding parties. The dramatic 'killing' of the Corn Spirit becomes understandable when one recalls the urgency and anxiety of bringing in the harvest, in a race against possible bad weather. George Ewart Evans has aptly called harvesting 'a quasi-military operation', 'an attack against an ancient enemy'. What surer way to raise morale and turn toil into competitive, aggressive sport than to personalize the 'enemy' into a Corn Spirit whom each worker wanted to 'kill'? Hence the jeers at laggards ('The Harvest Goat has butted him!', in Prussia) and at the man to cut the last sheaf ('You've killed the Cock!', in Poland); hence, too, the exuberant triumph when all is safely finished. Aggressive imagery comes spontaneously to the lips of men passionately engaged in hard work or in sport; the traditional jokes and tricks of the harvesters may have had less mysterious roots than Frazer supposed.

Frazer's work had an immense appeal to scholars and public alike, which is only now beginning to wane; *The Golden Bough* is certainly still the most famous discussion of mythology and folklore written in the English language. He has been uncritically admired and copied for so long that his theories have fed back into general public consciousness, and present-day perpetuators and revivers of folk customs in Western Europe often echo them. Among scholars, however, the pendulum is now swinging the other way. The reaction is a healthy one, yet among all the emphasis on the social and psychological functions of folk beliefs and folk customs, one must not lose sight of the fact that many of them were certainly perceived by the 'folk' themselves as attempts to grapple with supernatural problems. Even if one cannot prove, as

earlier scholars hoped, that mythological elements in folklore always derive from pre-Christian sources, they are of great intrinsic and historical interest, and each merits the most careful study possible from the available evidence. Even in Western Europe there is still untapped documentary evidence awaiting historians, as Ginzburg, Le Roy Ladurie, Henningsen, Keith Thomas and others have shown; in Eastern Europe, where modernization came

Above. Straw figure of a *Kornböcke*, a Swedish Harvest Goat. In many countries the corn-spirit was imagined as an animal, e.g. a cat, hare, goat, bull, horse or wolf, and the local corn dollies attempted to represent it realistically or by some allusion – in Wales, for instance, some dollies were plaited to look like a mare's tail. For a humanoid dolly, see Chapter One, p. 14.

Right. The 'Obby 'Oss at Padstow, Cornwall, 1922. A uniquely constructed 'horse', made of a round skirted frame with a head and tail fixed to the brim; it rests on the bearer's shoulders, his head being hidden by a mask and pointed hat.

slowly to many areas, much exciting fieldwork can still be done and, hopefully, made available in major languages. Traditional 'European Mythology' will soon be dead, though no doubt other systems of popular beliefs in the supernatural and the occult will arise to replace it and to co-exist, more or less uneasily, alongside Christianity. This book has been a brief attempt to explore some of its complexities.

Further Reading List

Alford, Violet, *The Hobby Horse and other Animal Masks*. Merlin Press, London, 1978.

Anderson, George K., *The Legend of the Wandering Jew*. Providence, Connecticut, 1965.

Ashe, Geoffrey (ed.), *The Quest for Arthur's Britain*. Pall Mall Press, London, 1968.

Baring-Gould, Sabine, *The Book of Werewolves*. New York, reprint, 1973.

Briggs, Katharine M., *The Vanishing People: A Study of Traditional Fairy Beliefs*. B. T. Batsford, London, 1978.

Briggs, Katharine M., *A Dictionary of British Folk-Tales in the English Language* (4 vols.). Routledge and Kegan Paul, London, 1970-71.

Brown, Theo, *The Fate of the Dead: Folk Eschatology in the West Country after the Reformation*. D. S. Brewer/Rowman and Littlefield, Cambridge and Towota, 1979.

Burke, Peter, *Popular Culture in Early Modern Europe*. London, 1978.

Cawte, E. C., *Ritual Animal Disguise*. D. S. Brewer/Rowman and Littlefield, Cambridge and Towota, 1978.

Cacciara, Guiseppe, *The History of Folklore in Europe*. Philadelphia, 1981.

Cohn, Norman, *Europe's Inner Demons*. Sussex University Press/Heinemann Educational Books, London and New York, 1975.

Dorson, R. M., *The British Folklorists: A History*. Routledge and Kegan Paul, London, 1968.

Ellworthy, F. T., *The Evil Eye*. London, 1895.

Frazer, Sir James G., *The Golden Bough*, abridged edn. Macmillan & Co., London, 1922.

Ginzburg, Carlo, *The Night Battles: Witchcraft and Agrarian Cults in the Sixteenth and Seventeenth Centuries*. Routledge and Kegan Paul, London, 1983.

Helm, Alex, *The Mummers' Play*. D. S. Brewer/Rowman and Littlefield, Ipswich and Towota, 1981.

Henningsen, Gustav, *The Witches' Advocate: Basque Witchcraft and the Spanish Inquisition*. University of Nebraska Press, Nebraska, 1980.

Jarman, A. O. J., *The Legend of Merlin*. University of Wales Press, Cardiff 1960.

Judge, Roy, *The Jack in the Green: A May Day Custom*. D. S. Brewer/Rowman and Littlefield, Cambridge and Towota, 1977.

Kligman, Gail, *Căluş: Symbolic Transformation in a Roumanian Ritual*. University of Chicago Press, Chicago, 1981.

Ladurie, E. Le Roy, *Montaillou: Cathars and Catholics in a French Village*. Scolar Press, London, 1978.

Loomis, C. G., *White Magic: An Introduction to the Folklore of Christian Legend*. Cambridge, Massachusetts, 1948.

Macfarlane, Alan D. J., *Witchcraft in Tudor and Stuart England*. Routledge and Kegan Paul, London and New York, 1970.

Mullen, Redmond, *Miracles and Magic*. A. R. Mowbray and Co., London and Oxford, 1978.

Palmer, P. M. and More, R., *The Sources of the Faust Tradition*. Oxford University Press, Oxford, 1936.

Pegg, Bob, *Rites and Riots: Folk Customs of Britain and Europe*. Blandford Press, London, 1981.

Porter, J. R., and Russell, W. M. S. (eds.), *Animals in Folklore*. D. S. Brewer/Rowman and Littlefield, Cambridge and Towota, 1978.

Rees, Alwyn and Brinley, *Celtic Heritage*. Thames and Hudson, London, 1961.

Russell, Jeffrey B., *A History of Witchcraft*. Thames and Hudson, London, 1980.

Schmitt, Jean-Claude, *The Holy Greyhound: Guinefort, Healer of Children*. Cambridge University Press, Cambridge, 1983.

Simpson, Jacqueline, *British Dragons*. B. T. Batsford, London, 1980.

Simpson, Jacqueline, *Legends of Icelandic Magicians*. D. S. Brewer/Rowman and Littlefield, Cambridge and Towota, 1975.

Summers, Montague, *The Werewolf*. Kegan Paul, London, 1933.

Thomas, Keith, *Religion and the Decline of Magic*. Weidenfeld and Nicolson, London and New York, 1971.

Thomson, David, *The People of the Sea*. Barrie and Rockliff, London and New York, 1965.

Ward, Donald, (ed. and transl.), *The German Legends of the Brothers Grimm*. Millington Books/Institute for the Study of Human Issues, London and New York, 1981.

Acknowledgments

Photographs. Alinari, Florence 33; Antikvarisk-topografiska arkivet, Stockholm 106; Ashmolean Museum, Oxford 84; BBC Hulton Picture Library, London 48 bottom, 81; Belgian National Tourist Office, London 26; Bibliothèque Nationale, Paris 83; Birmingham Museum and Art Gallery 69; Birmingham Public Libraries 13; Janet and Colin Bord, Corwen 7, 12, 23, 27, 51, 63, 73, 127; Janet and Colin Bord – Hamish M. Brown 15; Janet and Colin Bord – Fortean Picture Library 36 top, 52, 74, 102; Janet and Colin Bord – Margaret Ponting 30-31; Janet and Colin Bord – Anthony Weir 18; P. G. Boxhall 82; British Library, London 16, 17, 19, 22, 24, 88 top, 88 bottom, 92, 101, 108; J. Allan Cash Photolibrary, London 110; Castello Sforzesco, Milan 112; C. M. Dixon, Canterbury 75, 87; Mary Evans Picture Library, London 28, 107, 118 bottom, 126, 131; Photographie Giraudon, Paris 39, 56, 57 bottom, 58, 59, 70, 91, 103, 105; Hamlyn Group Picture Library 9, 36 bottom, 37, 41, 44, 57 top, 72 top, 72 bottom, 86, 93, 117 top, 122-123, 124 bottom, 128, 132, 136 top, 136 bottom, 140; Hamlyn Group – Curtis Lane and Company 90; Hereford City Museum 100; M. Holford, Loughton 2, 10-11, 14, 38, 46, 67, 71, 115, 135; Kirjandusmuuseum, Tartu 25 top; Leeds City Art Gallery 54-55; Mansell Collection, London 32, 60, 61, 68, 77, 78, 89, 116, 124 top, 136-137, 138-139, 141; Mas, Barcelona 42-43; Moravské Muzeum, Brno 114 left, 121; Museum and Art Gallery, Warrington 65; Museum Hameln 94-95; Muzeum Kroměřížska, Kroměříž – Miroslav Adamík 133; Muzeum Slaska Opolskiego, Opole 120; National Museum of Finland, Helsinki 8, 25 bottom, 118 top; National Museum of Ireland, Dublin 109; Néprajzi Múzeum, Budapest 29 top, 76, 96, 97; Nordiska Museet, Stockholm 64; Norfolk Museums Service, Norwich 134; Österreichische Nationalbibliothek, Vienna 21, 35; Österreichisches Museum für Volkskunde, Vienna 48 top, 117 bottom, 125 top, 125 bottom; Photoresources, Canterbury 98, 111; Rapho, Paris 130; Jean Ribière, Perpignan 129; Rijksmuseum Twenthe, Enschede 113; Royal Pavilion, Art Gallery and Museum, Brighton 53; Brian Shuel, London 31; Sotheby & Co, London 85; Staatliche Museum für Völkerkunde, Munich 29 bottom; Victoria and Albert Museum, London 40; Wellcome Historical Medical Museum, London 1, 104; T. Geoffrey Willey, Ponteland 114 right; D. C. Williamson, London 47; Roger Wood, London 45.

The photograph on page 13 is reproduced by permission of the Sir Benjamin Stone Collection, Birmingham Public Libraries.

Index